CAHSEE Study Guide
English-Language Arts

Publishing Information

CAHSEE Study Guide English-Language Arts

© 2008 California Department of Education.

Please note that any privately copyrighted reading passages contained in any CDE materials or on the CDE Web site may not be reproduced in publications for sale or otherwise. To obtain permission and terms of use for privately copyrighted materials, contact the copyright holder.

This printing of the *CAHSEE Study Guide English-Language Arts* contains the following privately copyrighted passages:

"A Day Away," from *Wouldn't Take Nothing for My Journey Now,* by Maya Angelou

"Reflections After the Rain," from *Navajo Voices and Visions Across the Mesa,* by Shonto Begay

"Early Spring," from *Navajo Voices and Visions Across the Mesa,* by Shonto Begay

"Slow Death of a Cave," from *Discover,* by Leslie Vreeland

A MESSAGE TO STUDENTS AND PARENTS

In 1999, California enacted a law requiring that every California public school student pass an examination to receive a high school diploma. The primary purpose of the California High School Exit Examination (CAHSEE) is to significantly improve pupil achievement in public high schools and to ensure that pupils who graduate from public high schools can demonstrate grade level competency in reading, writing, and mathematics. Since 1999 hundreds of thousands of students have taken and passed the CAHSEE. We realize that many students and their families find the prospect of taking this test stressful. Therefore, we are pleased to be able to provide students and their parents with this *English-Language Arts Study Guide*, which is designed to help students pass the CAHSEE.

The CAHSEE will be administered over two days. On the first day, students will take the English-language arts portion of the test; on the second day, they will take the mathematics portion. All of the questions on the CAHSEE are based on California's academic content standards in English-language arts and mathematics. These standards outline what students are expected to know and be able to do by the end of each school year from kindergarten through high school.

The focus of this study guide is the English-language arts part of the exam. It includes questions previously used on the CAHSEE and explains how to determine the correct answers. The guide also gives studying and test-taking tips and answers frequently asked questions. A similar study guide for mathematics is also available.

Passing the CAHSEE is an achievement for students, and we hope you find this guide helpful. If you have questions or would like more information about the CAHSEE, please contact your high school's principal or your school district's testing office. The California Department of Education's CAHSEE Web site at http://www.cde.ca.gov/ta/tg/hs/ is also an excellent resource.

Good luck with this exam!

Jack O'Connell

CALIFORNIA
DEPARTMENT OF
EDUCATION

JACK O'CONNELL
STATE SUPERINTENDENT OF PUBLIC INSTRUCTION

UN MENSAJE A LOS ALUMNOS Y SUS PADRES O GUARDIANES

En 1999, el estado de California pasó una ley que exige que todo alumno de una escuela pública de California apruebe un examen para recibir su diploma de preparatoria o high school. El propósito del examen es el de asegurar que los alumnos que se gradúen de la preparatoria o high school puedan leer y escribir en inglés y puedan usar las matemáticas.

Desde 1999 cientos de miles de estudiantes han tomado y han aprobado el CAHSEE. Nosotros estamos concientes de que el tener que tomar este examen es una fuente de tensión para los alumnos y sus familias. Por eso nos complace proveer a los alumnos y sus padres o guardianes con esta *Guía de Estudio de Inglés o English-Language Arts*, la cual esta diseñada para ayudar a los alumnos a prepararse para pasar el CAHSEE.

El CAHSEE se administra durante dos días. El primer día los alumnos tomarán la sección que se enfoca en los conocimientos de inglés o English-language arts. Durante el segundo día los alumnos tomarán la sección del examen que se enfoca en las matemáticas. Todas las preguntas del CAHSEE están basadas en los estándares estatales del contenido de inglés o English-language arts y de matemáticas. Estos estándares describen lo que se espera que los alumnos sepan y puedan hacer al final de cada año escolar desde el kinder hasta el 12° grado.

Esta guía de estudio se enfoca en la sección del examen que cubre los conocimientos **de inglés o English-language arts**. Incluye preguntas de exámenes previos y provee ayuda para determinar cual es la mejor respuesta; presenta estrategias para estudiar y para responder a preguntas; y responde a las preguntas más frecuentes acerca del examen. Existe una guía similar para la parte del examen que se concentra en matemáticas.

Pasar el CAHSEE es un gran logro para los alumnos y esperamos que esta guía les ayude. Si tiene preguntas o le gustaría obtener más información acerca del examen por favor llame al director de su escuela o a la oficina de evaluación de su distrito escolar. La página de Web del CAHSEE del Departamento de Educación de California también es un recurso excelente. Visítela en: http://www.cde.ca.gov/ta/tg/hs/.

¡Buena suerte con este examen!

Jack O'Connell

NOTE TO READER

We are pleased to present this revised student Study Guide to you. We have made several important changes based on the feedback we received from parents, students, teachers, and administrators. Focus groups from both northern and southern California analyzed the original Student Guides and provided suggestions to make them more useful and accessible to students. The following changes were made to the document:

- We have placed a full practice test in the beginning of the guide with an answer key in the appendix.
- Additional sample test questions have been added to both guides.
- Graphics and page design have been revised to improve readability.
- Mathematics and English-language arts now use consistent strategies to refer to content strands.
- Tabs have been added for easy reference to content strands.
- Explanations to the mathematics practice problems show dual approaches to solve each problem.
- Students are provided with strategies for solving English-language arts questions.

ACKNOWLEDGMENTS

We would like to thank Educational Testing Service (ETS), as well as the staff and students from San Bernardino High School and San Gorgonio High School in San Bernardino and C.K. McClatchy High School in Sacramento for their participation in our focus groups. Additionally, we would like to acknowledge the following CDE staff who provided input to this revised edition:

California Department of Education

Deb V. H. Sigman, Deputy Superintendent
Assessment and Accountability Branch

Tom Herman, Consultant
CAHSEE Office

Janet Chladek, Acting Director
Standards and Assessment Division

Bonnie Galloway, Consultant
CAHSEE Office

Diane Hernandez, Administrator
CAHSEE Office

Carrie Strong-Thompson, Consultant
CAHSEE Office

Much appreciation goes to the educators who contributed to the development of material provided in the original Study Guide.

Principal Author

Jane Hancock, Co-Director
California Writing Project, UCLA

Editor

Carol Jago, Co-Director
California Reading and Literature Project, UCLA
Teacher, Santa Monica High School
Santa Monica High School District

University of California
Office of the President

Elizabeth Stage, Director
Mathematics and Science
Professional Development

Harold Asturias, Deputy Director
Mathematics and Science
Professional Development

Susan Arnold, Assistant to the Director
Mathematics and Science
Professional Development

Advisory Panel

Karen Lopez, Teacher
William S. Hart High School
William S. Hart Union School District

Sidnie Myrick, Associate Director
California Writing Project, UCLA

Cynthia Oei, Teacher
Herbert Hoover High School
Glendale Unified School District

Tylene F. Quizon
Robert A. Millikan High School
Long Beach Unified School District

Anne Gani Sirota, Co-Director
California Reading and Literature Project, UCLA

Joyce Tamanaha-Ho, Teacher
Alhambra High School
Alhambra Unified School District

California Department of Education

Geno Flores, Former Deputy Superintendent
Assessment and Accountability Branch

Deb V.H. Sigman, Director
Standards and Assessment Division

Phil Spears, Former Director
Standards and Assessment Division

Lily Roberts, Former Administrator
CAHSEE Office

Janet Chladek, Former Administrator
CAHSEE Office

Terry Emmett, Administrator
Reading/Language Arts Leadership Office

Jessica Valdez, Consultant
CAHSEE Office

Bruce Little, Consultant
CAHSEE Office

Beth Brenneman, Consultant
Reading/Language Arts Leadership Office

Paul Michelson, Former Consultant
Testing and Reporting Office

Other Contributors

Meg Holmberg, Writing Consultant
EEPS Media

Tim Erickson, Writing Consultant
EEPS Media

Contents

Frequently Asked Questions

The following questions are often asked about the California High School Exit Examination (CAHSEE). If you have a question that is not answered here, call your high school's principal or your school district's testing office. You can find answers to other frequently asked questions on CDE's CAHSEE Web page, http://www.cde.ca.gov/ta/tg/hs/.

What does the CAHSEE cover?
The CAHSEE has two parts: English-language arts and mathematics.

The English-language arts part of the CAHSEE tests state content standards through grade ten. The reading section includes vocabulary, decoding, comprehension, and analysis of informational and literary texts. The writing section covers writing strategies, applications, and the conventions of standard English (for example, grammar, spelling, and punctuation).

The mathematics part of the CAHSEE tests state content standards in grades six and seven and Algebra I. The exam includes statistics, data analysis and probability, number sense, measurement and geometry, mathematical reasoning, and algebra. Students are also asked to demonstrate a strong foundation in computation and arithmetic, including working with decimals, fractions, and percentages.

What kinds of questions are on the CAHSEE?
Most of the questions on the CAHSEE are multiple choice. However, the English-language arts part of the exam also includes one essay question (writing task). The exam is given only in English, and all students must pass the exam in English to receive a high school diploma. Sample questions from previous administrations of the CAHSEE can be found throughout this Study Guide and on CDE's Web site.

When do students first take the CAHSEE?
Students must take the exam for the first time in the second part of their tenth grade year.

When (and how) do students find out whether they have passed the CAHSEE?
School districts receive student score reports about seven weeks after the date of the exam. One copy is to be mailed to the student's home and another copy is to be kept in the student's permanent record. It is important that parents or guardians keep a copy of the student report for their records. The State of California does *not* keep a copy of the scores. All individual student scores are confidential. Only group scores (for entire schools and districts) are made public. Scores may range from 275 to 450. A passing score is 350 or higher.

What if a student does not pass the first time?
Students who do not pass the exam in the tenth grade will have several opportunities to take it again during their junior and senior years. Once they have passed either part of the exam, they will not be tested again on that part. By state law, students who do not pass a part of the exam must be offered extra

instruction to learn what they need to know in order to pass. It is up to each school and district to decide how to provide this instruction. To find out what type of help is available and when the exam will be given again at your school, contact the principal or a counselor at your high school.

What if a student is a senior and still has not passed the CAHSEE?

Assembly Bill (AB347) states that you are entitled to receive intensive instruction and services for up to two consecutive academic years after completion of grade 12 or until you have passed both parts of the exit examination, whichever comes first. Also, you have the right to file a complaint regarding those services through the Uniform Complaint Procedure as set forth in California Education Code Section 35186.

What if a student has special needs?

If a student has an individualized education program (IEP) or a Section 504 Plan, it should describe any special arrangements the student is entitled to while taking an exam. Special arrangements for taking the CAHSEE are categorized as either "accommodations" or "modifications." It is important to understand the difference between them because it may affect a student's score on the exam.

> An **accommodation** does not alter what the test measures—for example, taking extra breaks during the exam or using a test booklet with large print.

> A **modification** fundamentally alters what the exam measures—for example, using a calculator on the mathematics part of the exam or hearing an audio presentation of the questions on the ELA part of the exam.

Students must be permitted to use any accommodations or modifications on the CAHSEE that are specified for testing purposes in their IEP or Section 504 Plan. Students who take the exam using an *accommodation* receive a score just as any other student does. However, students who use a *modification* receive a numeric score followed by the word "MODIFIED." If the student receives a score of 350 or higher, the student may be eligible for a waiver. This is done, in part, by presenting evidence proving that the student has gained the knowledge and skills otherwise needed to pass the CAHSEE.

More information about the procedure for requesting a waiver, including a list of modifications and accommodations, can be accessed on CDE's CAHSEE Web site or by talking with a high school principal.

What if a student is still learning to speak and read in English?

All students must pass the CAHSEE to be eligible for a high school diploma. Students who are English learners are required to take the CAHSEE in grade ten with all students. However, the law says that during their first 24 months in a California school, they are to receive six months of special instruction in reading, writing, and comprehension in English. Additionally, English learners must be permitted to take the CAHSEE with certain test variations if used regularly in the classroom. A student who does not pass the exam in grade ten will have additional opportunities to pass it.

Preguntas Hechas Frecuentemente

A continuación encontrará respuestas a las preguntas más frecuentes sobre el Examen *California High School Exit Examination* o CAHSEE. Si tiene preguntas cuyas respuestas no aparezcan aquí, por favor llame al director de su escuela o a la oficina de evaluación de su distrito escolar. Puede encontrar respuestas a otras preguntas frecuentes en la página de Web del Departamento de Educación de California o *CDE* y del CAHSEE http://www.cde.ca.gov/ta/tg/hs/.

¿Qué cubre el CAHSEE?

El CAHSEE tiene dos secciones: inglés y matemáticas.

La sección de inglés del CAHSEE cubre los estándares estatales del contenido abarcando hasta el décimo grado inclusive. La parte correspondiente a la lectura incluye vocabulario, decodificación, comprensión y análisis de textos de información y textos de literatura. En la parte de escritura, el examen cubre estrategias de la escritura, aplicaciones y las reglas del inglés (por ejemplo gramática, ortografía y puntuación).

La parte de matemáticas del CAHSEE cubre los estándares estatales del sexto y séptimo grado y álgebra I. El examen incluye estadística, análisis de datos y probabilidad, teoría de los números, medidas y geometría, razonamiento matemático y álgebra. Se espera que los alumnos demuestren tener destreza en cómputo y aritmética, incluyendo la habilidad de trabajar con decimales, fracciones y porcentajes.

¿Qué clase de preguntas contiene el CAHSEE?

La mayor parte de las preguntas en el CAHSEE son preguntas de selección múltiple. Sin embargo, la sección de inglés también incluye una pregunta en forma de ensayo (*writing task*). El examen se administra en inglés solamente y todos los alumnos deben aprobarlo en inglés para recibir su diploma de preparatoria o *high school*. En esta guía de estudio y en la página de Web del Departamento de Educación de California o *CDE*, hay ejemplos de preguntas que han aparecido en exámenes previos.

¿Cuándo toman los alumnos el CAHSEE por primera vez?

Los alumnos deberán tomar el examen por primera vez en la segunda parte de su décimo grado.

¿Cuándo (y cómo) sabrán los alumnos si aprobaron o no el CAHSEE?

Los distritos escolares reciben los reportes de las calificaciones obtenidas por sus alumnos aproximadamente siete semanas después de haber administrado el examen. Una copia se envía directamente a la casa del alumno y otra copia se archiva con el expediente permanente del alumno. Es importante que los padres o guardianes guarden una copia del reporte del alumno para sus archivos. El estado de California *no* retiene ninguna copia de los resultados. Los resultados de cada alumno son confidenciales. Se publican solamente resultados de grupos (de escuelas enteras y distritos). Las calificaciones varían entre los 275 a los 450 puntos. Se requiere una calificación de 350 o más para aprobar.

¿Qué pasa si un alumno no aprueba la primera vez?

Los alumnos que no aprueben el examen en el décimo grado tendrán varias oportunidades de tomarlo de nuevo durante el 11º y el 12º grado. Una vez que hayan aprobado una de las dos secciones del examen no tendrán que tomar esa parte de nuevo. La ley estatal exige que los alumnos que no aprueben alguna parte del examen reciban educación adicional que les ayude a aprender lo que necesitan saber para aprobarlo. Cada escuela y cada distrito decidirá cómo proveer esa educación adicional. Para saber que tipo de ayuda hay disponible en la escuela de su hijo o hija y cuando el examen será administrado de nuevo, llame al director o al consejero de la escuela.

¿Qué pasa si un alumno ya tiene el 12mo grado y todavía no ha aprobado una o ambas partes del CAHSEE?

La ley (AB 347) estatal establece que los alumnos quienes no han aprobado una ubno ambas partes del CAHSEE para el final del duodécimo grado tienen el derecho de recibir servicios e instrucción intensiva hasta dos años académicos consecutivos después de culminar el duodécimo grado o hasta aprobar ambas partes del CAHSEE, dependiendo de lo que ocurra primero. También, la ley estatal establece que usted tiene el derecho de remitir una queja si no tuvo la oportunidad de recibir estos servicios, o si los servicios ya mencionados no fueron adecuados. Si desea remitir una queja formal por favor de comunicarse con el administrador escolar.

¿Qué pasa si un alumno tiene necesidades especiales?

Si un alumno tiene un Programa de Estudios Individualizado o *individualized education program*—también conocido como IEP por sus siglas en inglés o un Plan de Sección 504, estos deberán describir los arreglos especiales a los que el alumno tiene derecho al tomar el examen.

Las dos clases de arreglos especiales para tomar el CAHSEE son "adaptaciones" y "modificaciones". Es importante entender la diferencia entre estas dos clases de arreglos porque pueden afectar la calificación que el alumno obtenga en el examen.

Una **adaptación** no altera lo que el examen evalúa—por ejemplo, tomar descansos adicionales durante el examen o usar un cuadernillo de examen con letras grandes.

Una **modificación** cambia fundamentalmente lo que el examen está evaluando—por ejemplo, usar una calculadora en la parte de matemáticas o escuchar una grabación de las preguntas en la sección de inglés.

Los alumnos tienen derecho a cualquier adaptación o modificación para tomar el CAHSEE que haya sido estipulada en su programa de IEP o plan de Sección 504. Los alumnos que tomen el examen usando una *adaptación* recibirán una calificación como todos los demás. Sin embargo, los alumnos que usen una *modificación* recibirán su calificación numérica seguida de la palabra "MODIFIED" (MODIFICADA). Sin embargo, si el alumno obtiene 350 puntos o más, el director de la escuela del alumno debe pedir a petición de los padres o guardianes una exención o *waiver* a la junta escolar de su localidad. Este proceso lleva a cabo, en parte, con una presentación para la junta escolar de su localidad, demostrando pruebas que el alumno ha adquirido los conocimientos y las destrezas necesarias que de otra manera sean necesarias para aprobar el CAHSEE.

Puede encontrar más información acerca del proceso para pedir esta exención o waiver incluyendo una lista de posibles adaptaciones y modificaciones en la página de Web del Departamento de Educación de California o hablando con el director de su escuela.

¿Qué pasa si un alumno todavía está aprendiendo a hablar y leer inglés?

Todos los alumnos deben pasar el CAHSEE para obtener su diploma de preporatoria o *high school*.

Los alumnos que están aprendiendo inglés o *English learners* tienen que tomar el CAHSEE en el décimo grado como todos los demás. Sin embargo, la ley exige que durante sus primeros 24 meses en una escuela de California deberán recibir seis meses de educación especializada en lectura, escritura y comprensión del inglés. Ademas, estudiantes de inglés como segunda lengua tienen que ser permitidos de tomar el CAHSEE con ciertas variaciones del examen si se usan regularmente en el salón de clase. Todo alumno que no apruebe el examen tendrá otras oportunidades para hacerlo.

Information for Students

This Study Guide has been written just for you. To receive a high school diploma, you must pass the CAHSEE, and we want to make sure you do.

The English-language arts part of the CAHSEE consists of 79 multiple-choice questions and one essay writing prompt. This Study Guide includes tips for answering the multiple-choice questions and responding to the writing prompt. Remembering these tips can help you pass the CAHSEE.

Tips for Preparing for the CAHSEE

❑ **Apply Yourself in the Classroom.**
The CAHSEE measures what you are learning and have already been taught in the classroom. More than any other preparation, attending your classes, paying attention in class, and doing your homework will help you pass the CAHSEE.

❑ **Get Help!**
If you have trouble understanding any part of your class work or this Study Guide, get help! Talk to a teacher, a counselor, your parents, your guardian, or students who have already passed the CAHSEE. Many students receive valuable help in study groups with other students.

Your school district offers special help for students who have not passed the exam. To find out what your school offers, ask your English teacher or principal.

❑ **Read for Fun!**
Reading for pleasure is one of the best ways to prepare. Most researchers agree that students who read for fun also improve their writing, grammar, spelling, and vocabulary.

❑ **Use this Study Guide**
Don't wait until the last minute. Find a place where it's easy to concentrate, and set aside some time each week to prepare. Starting early will ensure you have time to get help if you need it.

Tips for Using the Answer Document

❑ Use only a #2 pencil. Harder lead will be difficult to erase if you need to. Softer lead can leave smudges, and to the machine that scores the exam, a smudge can look the same as an answer you chose.

❑ Mark only one answer to each question. If you change an answer, erase the original answer completely.

❑ Be certain you are marking the right question on your answer document, especially if you skip a question you want to answer later.

Tips for Answering Multiple-Choice Questions

❑ **Relax!**
You don't have to answer every question correctly to pass the CAHSEE. If you become stressed, take a deep breath, relax, and focus on doing the best you can. You will have chances to retake the exam if you need to.

❑ **Take as Much Time as You Need.**
If you need extra time, you can keep working through the school day. Just tell the person administering the exam that you need more time.

❑ **Answer Easy Questions First.**
If a passage or question gives you trouble, skip it and focus on the ones that you understand. After you have answered the easy questions, return to the questions you skipped.

❑ **Make Notes in the Test Booklet (But <u>Not</u> on the Answer Document).**
Writing a note to yourself can help you think through a question. Also, if you skip a question and return to it, a record of your thinking will often help you understand a test question in a new way. As you read, you can underline, mark up the passage, and take notes in the test booklet.

❑ **Eliminate Answers You Know are Wrong.**
If you are not sure about the answer to a question, cross out any choices you *know* are wrong.

❑ **If You Must, Guess.**
On the CAHSEE, wrong answers do not count against you, so it is to your advantage to answer *every* question. Even if you guess, you have a one-out-of-four chance of answering correctly. If you can eliminate two out of the four choices in any question, you have a 50-50 chance of answering correctly.

❑ **Review Your Work!**
When you finish the last question, go back over the exam to review your thinking and correct any mistakes. If you guessed at a question, change your answer only if you have a good reason; often, your first instinct will be your best. Also, check your answer document for stray marks and erase them as cleanly as you can.

Tips for Answering Reading Passage Questions

Most of the multiple-choice questions follow a reading passage. Good readers and good test takers use these strategies.

❑ **Read the Questions Before Reading the Passage. Look for "Key Words."**
Key words express specific ideas and relationships between ideas. After you find key words in a question, see if you can find the same words in the passage. Underline them and pay special attention to the text around them.

❑ **Read the Entire Passage Before Answering the Questions that Follow.**
Some questions ask about general concepts rather than specific details in a passage. To answer these types of questions, you need to understand the passage as a whole.

❑ **Make Connections to Your Own Experience.**
Some questions ask you to interpret situations and draw conclusions. Making connections to your own knowledge and experiences can help you answer these types of questions. As you read, try to relate the passage to yourself and people you know.

Tips for Writing the Essay

You will be asked to write an essay for the English-language arts part of the CAHSEE. Good writers and good test takers use these strategies.

❑ **Read the Writing Prompt Carefully and Note the Key Words.**
The prompt will give you a topic, an audience, and a purpose for your writing. Before you begin writing, make sure you understand what the prompt is asking you to do.

❑ **Plan Before You Write.**
In your test booklet, make a list, an outline, a cluster, or a grid to help you get organized and stay on topic.

❑ **Proofread and Polish.**
You will have all of the time you need to not only organize your essay but to proofread and revise to clearly express your ideas.

English-Language Arts Practice Test

This is a practice test using sample CAHSEE questions to help you prepare for the CAHSEE. Answer all the questions in the practice test and then check your answers using the ANSWER KEY provided in the back.

When you take the actual CAHSEE, it will be separated into two sections. Session 1 will contain 21 multiple-choice questions and a writing task. Session 2 will contain 58 multiple-choice items. Remember that you may take as much time as you need within the regular school day, and you will have a break between Sessions 1 and 2.

This practice test is designed to familiarize you with the CAHSEE test format and the possible types of items you might see on the real test. Since this practice test contains only a few samples of each standard, it cannot be used to accurately predict how you will perform on the CAHSEE.

Becoming familiar with the test may be helpful, but the absolute best preparation for the English-language arts portion of the test is to read often, discuss what you read, and write about what you have read.

California High School Exit Examination

PRACTICE TEST

Read the following passage and answer questions 1 through 9.

A Day Away
By Maya Angelou

Most people today know Maya Angelou as one of America's most important poets. One of her stories, "Georgia, Georgia," was the first story by an African-American woman to be made into a television movie. Angelou also wrote the screenplay for the movie *All Day Long* and even directed it. The variety, quality, and passion of her work continue to inspire people today.

1   We often think that our affairs, great or small, must be tended continuously and in detail, or our world will disintegrate, and we will lose our places in the universe. That is not true, or if it is true, then our situations were so temporary that they would have collapsed anyway.

2   Once a year or so I give myself a day away. On the eve of my day of absence, I begin to unwrap the bonds which hold me in harness. I inform housemates, my family and close friends that I will not be reachable for twenty-four hours; then I disengage the telephone. I turn the radio dial to an all-music station, preferably one which plays the soothing golden oldies. I sit for at least an hour in a very hot tub; then I lay out my clothes in preparation for my morning escape, and knowing that nothing will disturb me, I sleep the sleep of the just.

3   On the morning I wake naturally, for I will have set no clock, nor informed my body timepiece when it should alarm. I dress in comfortable shoes and casual clothes and leave my house going no place. If I am living in a city, I wander streets, window-shop, or gaze at buildings. I enter and leave public parks, libraries, the lobbies of skyscrapers, and movie houses. I stay in no place for very long.

4 On the getaway day I try for amnesia. I do not want to know my name, where I live, or how many dire responsibilities rest on my shoulders. I detest encountering even the closest friend, for then I am reminded of who I am, and the circumstances of my life, which I want to forget for a while.

5 Every person needs to take one day away. A day in which one consciously separates the past from the future. Jobs, family, employers, and friends can exist one day without any one of us, and if our egos permit us to confess, they could exist eternally in our absence.

6 Each person deserves a day away in which no problems are confronted, no solutions searched for. Each of us needs to withdraw from the cares which will not withdraw from us. We need hours of aimless wandering or spaces of time sitting on park benches, observing the mysterious world of ants and the canopy of treetops.

7 If we step away for a time, we are not, as many may think and some will accuse, being irresponsible, but rather we are preparing ourselves to more ably perform our duties and discharge our obligations.

8 When I return home, I am always surprised to find some questions I sought to evade had been answered and some entanglements I had hoped to flee had become unraveled in my absence.

9 A day away acts as a spring tonic. It can dispel rancor, transform indecision, and renew the spirit.

From WOULDN'T TAKE NOTHING FOR MY JOURNEY NOW by Maya Angelou, copyright © 1993 by Maya Angelou. Used by permission of Random House, Inc.

64B

1. **The words *casual*, *wander*, and *gaze* in Paragraph 3 suggest a feeling of—**

   A determination.

   B solitude.

   C bewilderment.

   D relaxation.

   L164B006

2. **What is the narrator's main purpose in this passage?**

   A to entertain readers with a story of an unusual day

   B to inform readers how to organize a day away from home

   C to persuade readers to take some time for themselves

   D to describe to readers what it is like to rediscover a city

   L164B007

3. **Which statement from the passage BEST describes the narrator's motivation for "a day away"?**

    A . . . we will lose our places in the universe.

    B . . . I sleep the sleep of the just.

    C . . . I want to forget for a while.

    D . . . friends can exist one day without any one of us.

    L164B009

4. **The narrator MOST likely laid out her clothes the night before her day away so that she—**

    A wouldn't forget what she wanted to wear.

    B wouldn't have to make a decision in the morning.

    C would be able to sleep late in the morning.

    D would be as stylishly dressed as possible.

    L164B010

5. **Which of the following is the main theme of the passage?**

    A Self-energizing oneself is necessary.

    B Time is of the essence.

    C Problems will solve themselves.

    D A single decision has many consequences.

    L164B011

6. **Which sentence below is an example of a simile?**

    A I will have set no clock . . .

    B I do not want to know my name . . .

    C We need hours of aimless wandering . . .

    D A day away acts as a spring tonic.

    L164B013

7. **Which sentence from the passage is an example of figurative language?**

    A Once a year or so I give myself a day away.

    B On the eve of my day of absence, I begin to unwrap the bonds which hold me in harness.

    C I enter and leave public parks, libraries, the lobbies of skyscrapers, and movie houses.

    D It can dispel rancor, transform indecision, and renew the spirit.

    L164B014

8. **In which sentence from the passage does the narrator acknowledge those who disagree with her main argument?**

   A I inform housemates, my family and close friends that I will not be reachable for twenty-four hours; then I disengage the telephone.

   B I detest encountering even the closest friend, for then I am reminded of who I am, and the circumstances of my life, which I want to forget for a while.

   C If we step away for a time, we are not, as many may think and some will accuse, being irresponsible, but rather we are preparing ourselves to more ably perform our duties and discharge our obligations.

   D When I return home, I am always surprised to find some questions I sought to evade had been answered and some entanglements I had hoped to flee had become unraveled in my absence.

   L164B015

9. **Which BEST describes the narrator's tone in the second half of the passage?**

   A persuasive

   B humorous

   C sarcastic

   D frustrated

   L164B016

Read the following passage and answer questions 10 through 15.

The Remarkable Paper Cuttings of Hans Christian Andersen

1 Best known as an author of fairy tales, Hans Christian Andersen wrote such children's classics as "The Ugly Duckling," "The Little Mermaid," and "The Emperor's New Clothes." Many people may not be aware, however, that he was also an actor, a singer, and an artist, and that as an artist, he excelled at the unusual craft of paper cutting.

2 Andersen may have begun practicing paper cutting as a young boy in Denmark. It is known that he loved to play with puppets and frequently created clothes for them from scraps of cloth. He also may have helped cut leather for his father, a shoemaker. These practices could have contributed to his proficiency in using scissors to create works of art.

3 Paper cutting was not a well-known craft in Denmark during the 1800s. Some Europeans created silhouettes out of black paper, but Andersen's cuttings were quite different. Andersen usually used white or brightly colored paper. He never drew an outline first but simply snipped away with a design that existed only in his imagination.

Sometimes he used a flat piece of paper. Other times he folded the paper, made some cuts, opened the paper, and then refolded it in a different way before cutting again. When at last he unfolded the finished paper cutting, an intricate design could be seen, often incorporating dancers, swans, windmills, storks, and castles. Frequently, the images were bordered by a stage with curtains and fancy decorations.

4 Andersen had many reasons for making his paper cuttings, but the main one was to entertain. Andersen loved to tell his fanciful stories to anyone who would listen. As he spoke, he would take out his scissors and create a remarkable paper cutting to illustrate his words. Audiences remained enthralled as they awaited the end of the tale and the outcome of the mysteriously changing piece of paper. Books, especially those other than instructional, were not very common at the time. People who enjoyed hearing a story purely for the sake of entertainment valued Andersen's unique skill as a storyteller and an artist.

5   Andersen also found that his paper cuttings helped bridge a communication gap between himself and others. Although an awkward and shy man, Andersen still loved an audience. His stories and paper cuttings helped him to communicate when he would have otherwise felt uncomfortable. He loved to travel and always took his scissors along. When encountering those who spoke different languages, Andersen found he could always make a connection by demonstrating his beautiful paper creations.

6   The paper cuttings also became unique gifts for friends and family. Sometimes Andersen would paste the cuttings into scrapbooks and present them to the children of relatives. Other times they were given as tokens of appreciation to hosts and hostesses. When his writing brought him fame, these gifts were even more valued.

7   Now more than 100 years old, many of Andersen's delicate paper cuttings still exist in a museum in Denmark devoted to his work. While Andersen will always be remembered for his classic fairy tales, his beautiful works of art also remain for all to enjoy.

02B

10. **Which is the BEST way to summarize the information about Hans Christian Andersen in the first paragraph?**

   A   Everyone has read a book written by Hans Christian Andersen.

   B   Hans Christian Andersen was gifted in the art of paper cutting.

   C   Hans Christian Andersen was active in other areas of the arts.

   D   People remember Hans Christian Andersen for more than one talent.

L102B002

11. **Based on the information in the passage, which of the following is MOST likely to happen?**

   A   Andersen's paper cuttings will be preserved for many years.

   B   The museum will replace the paper cuttings with other objects created by Andersen.

   C   Interest in Andersen's books will diminish when people learn about his paper cuttings.

   D   Andersen's paper cuttings will become more treasured than his writings.

L102B003

California High School Exit Examination

PRACTICE TEST

12. This passage provides the LEAST information on which topic related to Hans Christian Andersen?

   A the reason he liked paper cutting

   B why he became proficient at paper cutting

   C the museum devoted to his work

   D the process he used to make his designs

L102B004

13. According to the information in the passage, which phrase describes both Andersen's published stories and his paper cuttings?

   A given as gifts

   B used to entertain

   C famous worldwide

   D created for children

L102B011

14. Which of the following would make this passage easier to understand?

   A a picture of one of Andersen's paper cuttings

   B an excerpt from one of Andersen's fairy tales

   C a quote from someone who owns one of Andersen's paper cuttings

   D an explanation of what inspired Andersen to write fairy tales for children

L102B013

15. What is the main purpose of this passage?

   A to illustrate the importance of having a variety of skills

   B to compare entertainment of the past to that of the present

   C to illustrate how a person used art to overcome shyness

   D to explore a lesser-known talent of a famous writer

L102B014

California High School Exit Examination

PRACTICE TEST

Read the following poem and answer questions 16 through 18.

Reflections After the Rain

By Shonto Begay

Little tadpoles dart around my feet

as I stand ankle deep in water

after a brief, but hard summer rainstorm.

The earth smells fresh and delicious.

5   Fragrance of wet sand always washes away worries.

Distant drifting clouds reflect in the pond

like friendly puffy giants spreading happiness.

In the distance, goat bells tinkle,

letting us know they are near.

10   My mother sits with her feet in the water,

in silent thoughts of thankfulness.

The water holes are full once again.

We do not have to take the flock

a half day's walk up to the windmill.

15   Tadpoles tickle my ankles, and I laugh.

On days of no rain my mother tells me stories

as we walk the herd up to the mesa,

stories of the land and stories of her childhood.

They are always welcome.

20   The dogs bark and bells rattle loudly.

Something has startled the flock.

High above against the breaking clouds

a solitary raven appears.

It is time to move the sheep and

25   the goats back toward home.

I squish my toes into the soft muddy

bottom of the pond, and the tadpoles scatter.

The earth smells delicious.

We are thankful for the rain.

From NAVAJO VOICES AND VISIONS ACROSS THE
MESA by Shonto Begay. Copyright, 1995 by Shonto Begay.
Reprinted by permission of Scholastic Inc.

25C

16. **Which term BEST describes the relationship between the speaker and his mother?**

    A aloof

    B doting

    C amiable

    D awkward

    L225C005

17. **Which of these is a flashback in the poem?**

    A The earth smells fresh and delicious

    B The water holes are full once again

    C On days of no rain my mother tells me stories

    D Something has startled the flock

    L225C012

18. **The poem MOST imparts a feeling of—**

    A pride.

    B joy.

    C tenderness.

    D peacefulness.

    L225C016

California High School Exit Examination

PRACTICE TEST

Read the following article and answer questions 19 through 21.

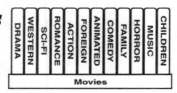

Main Street Movies Employee Manual: Organizing Videos

In order to help customers find what they want quickly and to keep track of inventory, it's important to keep the thousands of titles in the Main Street Movies store organized properly. This section of the *Employee Manual* will tell you how to organize videos so that customers will always be able to find them. It will also help you familiarize yourself with the store layout, so that you can help a customer find a particular film or a particular genre of film.

Each Main Street Movies store has three main sections:

       1. New Releases Wall
       2. Film Library
       3. Video Games

New Releases Wall. Almost 70 percent of movie rentals are new releases, and that is the first place that most customers go when they

enter the store. The center section of shelves on this wall holds **Hottest Hits**. When new titles come into the store (about 40 per month), place them on this wall in alphabetical order.

After 30 days, move the Hottest Hits titles to the shelves on either side, again in alphabetical order. The shelves flanking Hottest Hits are called **Recent Releases**. Titles stay on the Recent Releases shelves eight to ten months before being moved to Film Library shelves. The New Releases Wall, including the Hottest Hits and Recent Releases shelves, holds about 350 titles.

Film Library. The thousands of titles in the Film Library are organized into categories (genres). The films within each category are displayed alphabetically. Here are the categories and their two-letter computer codes:

California High School Exit Examination

PRACTICE TEST

AC	Action	FA	Family	SC	Science Fiction
CH	Children	FL	Foreign Language*	SI	Special Interest
CL	Classics	FO	Foreign	WE	Western
CO	Comedy	HO	Horror		
DR	Drama	MU	Music		

*Foreign Language titles include films that were originally made in a foreign language, films that have been dubbed into a foreign language, and films with foreign language subtitles. A sticker on the back of each box specifies which type of film it is.

Special Interest includes these sub-categories:

AN	Animation	IN	Instruction	SP	Sports
DO	Documentaries	RE	Religion	TR	Travel
EX	Exercise				

Video Games. Main Street Movies carries games for Super Nintendo, Sony Play Station, and Nintendo 64 game systems. Games for all three systems are arranged together, in alphabetical order.

Although video games represent only a small percentage of our inventory, they are shoplifted more often than any other type of merchandise in our store. Therefore, video games are *never* displayed on the shelves. Shelves in the Video Game section of Main Street Movies hold cardboard plaques with pictures and information about each game. When a customer wants to rent a particular game, he or she will bring you the plaque. You then retrieve the game from the locked case behind the counter, rent it to the customer, and file the cardboard plaque in the "Video Game Rentals" box. When the game is returned, put the plaque back on the appropriate shelf so that it is available for another customer.

077

19. What is the order in which new movies are moved through the store?

A from Hottest Hits to Film Library to Recent Releases

B from Film Library to Hottest Hits to Recent Releases

C from Hottest Hits to Recent Releases to Film Library

D from Recent Releases to Film Library to Hottest Hits

L0077001

20. Which of the following is NOT a subcategory of Special Interest?

A Animation

B Exercise

C Religion

D Western

L0077002

21. A customer wants to know if a Foreign Language video has subtitles. Based upon the manual, what is the best way to find this information?

A Look at the back of the box.

B Check the computer.

C Ask an employee.

D Watch a few minutes of the film.

L0077004

California High School Exit Examination

PRACTICE TEST

Read the following poem and answer questions 22 through 25.

Early Spring

By Shonto Begay

In the early spring, the snowfall is light

upon the mesa.

It does not stick to the ground very long.

I walk through this patchwork of snow and earth,

5   watching the ground for early signs.

Signs of growth. Signs of rebirth.

Larkspur and wild onions are still

within the warmth of the earth.

I hear cries of crows off in the distance.

10 A rabbit bounds off into the sagebrush flat.

A shadow of a hawk disturbs the landscape momentarily.

It sees food and life abundant below that I cannot see.

The cycle of life continues.

Even as I stand here shivering in the afternoon chill,

15 just below me, young seedlings start

their upward journey.

Insects begin to stir.

Rodents and snakes are comfortable in their burrows.

California High School Exit Examination

PRACTICE TEST

Maybe to them we also disappear with the cold.

20 Not to be seen until spring.

For this generation, and many more to come,

this land is beautiful and filled with mysteries.

They reveal themselves and their stories—

if you look very carefully, and listen . . .

From NAVAJO VOICES AND VISIONS ACROSS THE MESA by Shonto Begay. Copyright © 1995 by Shonto Begay. Reprinted by permission of Scholastic Inc.

24C

22. **The poet's purpose in writing this poem is MOST likely to encourage people to—**

A take part in conservation efforts.

B pay attention to nature.

C travel to nature reserves.

D think about the changes of season.

L224C006

23. **Which line from the poem looks MOST to the future?**

A Signs of growth. Signs of rebirth

B just below me, young seedlings start

C Not to be seen until spring

D For this generation, and many more to come

L224C009

24. **What is distinctive about Lines 19 and 20 of the poem?**

A They consider a different point of view.

B They look to the past rather than the present.

C They refer to a different topic from the other lines.

D They contradict the overall message of the poem.

L224C013

25. **The point of view of the poem is that of—**

A a human at ground level.

B a bird flying through the sky.

C the plants growing in the earth.

D the earth preparing for growth.

L224C014

Read the following article and answer questions 26 through 31.

Pro and Con on Vitamin Supplements

Pro: The Key to a Long and Healthy Life

1   No medical breakthrough means so much, to so many people, as the discovery of the role of nutrition in human health and longevity. Numerous scientific studies have shown that specific nutrients hold the key to a strong heart and cardiovascular system, a healthy immune system, a normal nervous system, and more. They can help prevent cancer, loss of memory and vision, physical and mental defects in newborns, and degeneration of health in seniors. Vitamins and minerals are essential to the healthy function of every system within our bodies; without them we would not have the energy to perform even the simplest daily task.

2   Perhaps the most important part of any healthy diet, therefore, is a nutritional supplement. The simple "vitamin"—a comprehensive formula of high-quality, high-potency vitamins and minerals—is a sure source of nutrition that can lead to better health, a longer life, and a better quality of life for years to come.

3   Those who recommend against a daily supplement, relying on a balanced diet instead, are unrealistic and uninformed. Few people consume the right amounts or types of foods to meet the recommended daily intake of vitamins and minerals. To get a full day's supply of calcium, for example, you'd have to consume 1 cup of milk, PLUS 1 cup of chopped broccoli, PLUS one cup of navy beans, PLUS one cup of plain yogurt, PLUS four ounces of canned pink salmon.

4   The U.S. Department of Agriculture's (USDA's) Food Guide Pyramid recommends eating 2-3 servings each of meats and dairy products, 2-4 servings of fruits, 3-5 servings of vegetables, and 6-11 servings of breads, cereals, rice, and

other grains every day. Most people don't meet those guidelines. Some groups in particular, such as senior citizens, find it hard to squeeze that many servings into their daily diets. In a special food guide pyramid modified to address the needs of older Americans, the Tufts University USDA Human Nutrition Research Center specifically recommends supplements of calcium, vitamin D, and vitamin B12, vitamins many older adults find difficult to get in adequate amounts from food alone.

5   Even people who get the recommended number of servings may not get the nutrition they expect. In this world of fast and processed food, little nutritive value is left in the food we eat. On top of that, many essential nutrients, such as vitamin C and the energy-producing B vitamins, are water-soluble. Because they are not stored in the body, adequate amounts must be consumed every single day. A supplement is like nutritional insurance. It fills the nutritional gap between the foods you eat and the amount you need. But even if you could meet the recommended daily values for every nutrient every day, would that be enough for vibrant good health? Probably not. Scientific studies show that some vitamins and minerals can fight the aging

process and strengthen your immune system—but only at levels far higher than the recommended daily value. Only through supplementation can you regularly and reliably get the high potencies needed for optimal good health.

6   Today, good nutrition is as close as the grocery store shelf. Help yourself to a daily vitamin and mineral supplement, and help yourself to improved health and longevity.

Con: Danger in Disguise

7   Today, we know that the role of vitamins and minerals goes way beyond the prevention of deficiency diseases, such as scurvy, to actually preventing cancer and heart disease, the most fearsome and ferocious killers of our time. With this knowledge has come the widespread call for nutritional supplementation—and a confusing array of vitamin, mineral, and herbal supplements lining the supermarket shelves.

8   Far from contributing to better health, however, nutritional supplements threaten to turn a scientific breakthrough into a nutritional disaster.

9   Promoters of vitamins and minerals—especially the antioxidant vitamins A, C, and E—would have consumers believe that the little vitamin pill in the bottle is all they need for good health. Take your vitamins in the morning, and you're covered. It's okay to eat fast foods for the rest of the day or skip meals to achieve today's fashionably skinny look. But vitamins and minerals are only one part of the nutritional puzzle. A diet rich in fiber and balanced in carbohydrates and protein is essential for good health. You can't get these things from a nutritional supplement. The focus on vitamin and mineral supplements may actually be robbing us of the full nutrition we seek.

10   And no supplement can compare to the quality of nutrition found in natural sources. For example, our bodies convert carotenes from plant foods into vitamin A. Many supplements contain a single carotene, beta-carotene. Natural sources are rich in many different carotenes, many of which are much more potent antioxidants than beta-carotene. Many supplements contain a synthetic form of vitamin E, when natural vitamin E is more readily absorbed and used by the body. And science is still discovering the wealth of nutrients in foods, including oligomeric proanthocyanidins (OPCs) found in grapes. These antioxidants are up to 50 times more powerful than Vitamin E and are efficiently used by the body.

11   You'd be hard-pressed to find a supplement as nutritionally comprehensive and potent as a balanced diet. Even if you could, you'd pay much more than if you got the same nutritional value from natural sources.

12   But perhaps the greatest danger presented by nutritional supplements comes from the very real risks presented by self-medication. Anyone can walk into the market and buy as many different supplements as desired. The reported benefits of high dosages of certain nutrients have led some people to believe that the more the better. Many take several vitamin and mineral supplements without regard to total intake or possible interactions.

13   High-dose supplements of vitamin A can cause toxicity, leading to bone fractures,

joint pain, liver failure, and other significant symptoms. Excess vitamin D can result in kidney damage. Too much vitamin K can interfere with anti-clotting medications. Because these fat-soluble vitamins can be stored in the body, where excess amounts can build up to dangerous levels, experts recommend supplementation only with a doctor's supervision.

14 Surprising new research suggests that vitamin C pills may speed up hardening of the arteries, the underlying cause of heart attacks and strokes. Researchers said their findings support the recommendations of health organizations, which urge people to avoid high doses of supplements and to get their nutrients from food instead.

15 As appealing as they're made to sound, nutritional supplements are danger in disguise. If you're looking for good health, don't look on the supplement shelves of your supermarket. Look in the produce section instead.

078

26. **The USDA Human Nutrition Research Center probably recommends calcium and other supplements for older adults because they—**

A drink less vitamin-enriched milk than they should.

B may lack the appetite to eat as many servings of food as are needed daily for a sufficient intake of minerals and vitamins.

C eat mostly processed food and fast food.

D may be more eager than younger adults to experiment with vitamins and minerals to improve the quality and longevity of their lives.

L0078004

27. **Read this sentence from the article.**

> A supplement is like nutritional insurance.

What does the author mean by comparing the use of supplements to insurance?

A Like nutritional supplements, insurance is necessary in order to maintain good health.

B Having insurance and using supplements will keep bad health away.

C Both insurance and vitamins are important in curing health problems.

D Like insurance, the nutritional value of supplements will be available when you need it.

L0078005

28. **Based on the second article, which of these statements is true?**

A Vitamin supplements provide adequate carotenes for the human body.

B A mineral supplement may be as full of nutrients as a balanced diet.

C Vitamin supplements are less valuable than eating a variety of healthy foods.

D A surplus of vitamin supplements can be beneficial to some people.·

L0078008

29. **What information supports the idea that vitamin supplements are potentially dangerous?**

A Supplements are usually available in powder, tablet, and liquid form.

B People might accidentally take supplements that interfere with medications.

C Supplements may play a large role in disease prevention.

D People tend to be too cautious when using supplements.

L0078009

California High School Exit Examination

PRACTICE TEST

30. Instead of depending heavily on vitamin supplements, the author of the second article encourages readers to—

A   eat fruits and vegetables.

B   begin an exercise program.

C   skip meals when necessary.

D   limit the intake of protein.

L0078010

31. Read this sentence from the article.

> Help yourself to a daily vitamin and mineral supplement, and help yourself to improved health and longevity.

What does this sentence mean?

A   Helping others means encouraging them to take vitamins and minerals.

B   A large helping of vitamins and minerals is necessary for good health.

C   Taking vitamins and minerals is one way that people may help themselves.

D   Taking vitamins and minerals regularly will have a positive effect on a person's health.

L0078010

PRACTICE TEST

Read the following poem and answer questions 32 through 36.

I've Watched . . .

I've watched the white clouds pantomime
The inner workings of my mind,
Where thought and feeling paint a scene
As if the blue sky were a dream.

5 I've watched the snow-bogged trees bend down
And shake their coats upon the ground
In order that they may reclaim
A straighter truth from whence they came.

I've watched the congress of the geese
10 Assemble in a perfect V
In order that they may keep sight
Of one another's path of flight.

I've watched the flood tide turn its head
And slack before the coming ebb
15 Without want or predilection
Waiting for the moon's direction.

I've watched the ocean lashed by wind,
Make a fool of the fishermen,
Who thought their knowledge of the sea
20 Ensured them some security.

But all this watching, knows not much,
For what are wind and sea and such,
The V of geese, the bent-down tree,
If nothing more than mystery?

04A

32. **What is the theme of the poem?**

   A   Clouds can be a reflection of our thoughts.

   B   Geese assemble in the shape of a V to navigate properly.

   C   Nature remains a mystery, regardless of our observations.

   D   Trees often bend beneath the weight of the snow.

   L104A002

33. **As used in the first two lines, what does *pantomime* mean?**

   > I've watched the white clouds pantomime/ The inner workings of my mind,

   A   move

   B   mock

   C   dramatize

   D   influence

   L104A003

34.

   > I've watched the ocean lashed by wind,

   In this line from the poem, the word *lashed* suggests that the ocean is being—

   A   soothed.

   B   troubled.

   C   sailed.

   D   whipped.

   L104A005

35. **Which phrase BEST represents the organization of the poem?**

   A   5 stanzas about nature and 1 about people

   B   5 stanzas of observation and 1 of conclusion

   C   1 stanza of introduction and 5 of explanation

   D   1 stanza about poetry and 5 about nature

   L104A007

36. **According to Lines 17–20, the fishermen's knowledge of the sea—**

   A   reflects their love of natural elements.

   B   helps them navigate more effectively.

   C   is greater than their knowledge of the weather.

   D   does not guarantee them safety.

   L104A009

California High School Exit Examination

PRACTICE TEST

Read the following brochure and answer questions 37 through 41.

Santa Lucia Scenic Trail
A Multi-Purpose Trail

The Trail

1   The Santa Lucia Scenic Trail is a network of over 50 miles of multi-purpose trails for hikers, runners, walkers, cyclists, and horseback riders. Currently, both paved and unpaved trails wind along the Pacific Coast, where the variety of natural wonders is unsurpassed in beauty. More trails are planned, and they will be built as funds become available.

The History

2   A combination hiking and biking trail had long been a dream of Carlos Ventura, a lifelong cyclist and resident of San Luis Obispo, California. For years, he was an advocate for more alternative means of transportation, especially recreational bicycle paths. In 1990, paving the way for Ventura's dream, local officials from Cambria and Morro Bay approached the California Department of Natural Resources to acquire an abandoned railroad right-of-way[1] that ran

---

[1]**railroad right-of-way:** a piece of land on which railroad tracks are built

along the California coast, citing the need for an alternative means of transportation. After numerous public hearings and multiple engineering plans, the Federal Highway Administration (FHA) approved the final plan in 1999.

3   With a grant from the FHA, the communities of Cambria and Morro Bay and the California Department of Natural Resources worked together to provide 100% funding for the trail. The first section of the trail was dedicated on August 15, 2001, as a multi-purpose trail for walkers, hikers, runners, cyclists, and horseback riders. That same day, the Santa Lucia

Scenic Trail Association (SLSTA) was formed with the following objectives:

- expand and maintain existing trails

- encourage trail etiquette

- educate users so that everyone enjoys a safe visit along the trail

4   The main trail is a 20-mile, paved multi-purpose trail that runs along the old railroad right-of-way. Two unpaved paths branch off for those who ride horses. More branches of paved and unpaved trails are planned, including trails for cyclists and hikers. Trail maps created by the SLSTA are available at the Welcome Center.

Trail Etiquette

5   The SLSTA guidelines have been established to ensure cooperation of multiple users: walkers, hikers, runners, cyclists, and horseback riders. Remember that each user has equal rights to the trail. To ensure these rights, please respect the following trail etiquette:

- Only non-motorized forms of transportation are permitted.*

---

*Persons using motorized wheelchairs are allowed access to paved trails.

- Cyclists yield to foot traffic; all users yield to horses.

- Cyclists keep right of the trail, except to pass; announce "on your left" when passing; and move off paved trail when stopped.

- Keep pets on leash and clean up after them.

- Carry out everything that is carried onto the trails.

- Camping is prohibited. Contact park ranger for nearest camping facilities.

Trail Safety Tips

6   To ensure a safe visit, users need to assess their limits and abilities before starting out on a trail. Public phones are located at the main entrance and at the end of the trail; however, there are no public phones along the trail (an emergency phone system has not yet been installed). To ensure everyone's safety, please review these tips:

- Tell someone your destination and trail before setting out.

- Wear clothing appropriate for the weather.

California High School Exit Examination

PRACTICE TEST

- Carry a flashlight and wear reflective clothing before sunrise and after sunset.

- If you are cycling, check equipment, wear a helmet, carry a tire pump, and maintain a safe speed.

- Use caution around horses.

Problems, Suggestions, Comments

7   To better serve users, the SLSTA welcomes all helpful comments or suggestions. If you notice something that needs attention or someone who is acting in an unsafe manner, do not hesitate to contact the Park Ranger. You can also leave a detailed note at the Welcome Center.

8   If you would like to join SLSTA, visit the Welcome Center and sign up. It's free! Plus, you will receive SLSTA's monthly newsletter by e-mail, containing articles by members and SLSTA staff. Paper copies are available for those without access to e-mail.

Support

9   There are no admission fees for use of the trails. SLSTA relies on donations to avoid charging trail users. Visit the Welcome Center or write SLSTA, P.O. Box 31, Cambria, CA 90228.

Emergency

10   Dial 911 for police.

Trail Hours

11   Open daily, dawn to dusk.

01B

37. **In the excerpt below, what is meant by the phrase *paving the way for Ventura's dream*?**

> In 1990, paving the way for Ventura's dream, local officials from Cambria and Morro Bay approached the California Department of Natural Resources to . . .

A   making a sidewalk for Ventura

B   allowing Ventura's idea to proceed

C   covering Ventura's trail with asphalt

D   considering the value of Ventura's plan

L101B001

38. **The phrase *trail etiquette* suggests that trail users—**

A   will dress in the appropriate fashion.

B   might have many choices of trails.

C   must avoid dangerous maneuvers.

D   should be considerate of other users.

L101B002

39. Which of the following information would be MOST helpful to include in the brochure for users of the trail?

A a biography of Carlos Ventura

B a list of the nearest convenience stores

C a map showing the location of the trails

D a directory of volunteers who work on the trail

L101B013

40. What is a benefit of becoming a member of SLSTA?

A Members will be given free access to all trails.

B Members will be allowed to camp along the trail.

C Members will be permitted to bring friends on trails.

D Members will receive a newsletter on trail-related topics.

L101B015

41. According to the information in the section entitled "Trail Safety Tips," what should hikers do before starting out?

A Always carry a warm jacket.

B Use caution around horses.

C Learn the location of public phones along the trail.

D Inform someone else which trail the hiker will use.

L101B003

Read the following passage and answer questions 42 through 45.

A Universal Language

1 Thousands of different languages exist in the world, some spoken by millions of people and some spoken by only a few. Since it is difficult and time-consuming to learn a new language, many people speak only one. Some people have a little knowledge of one or two other languages but aren't able to put them into practice very often. Travelers to foreign countries often have to rely on a translator or an international dictionary. Wouldn't it be helpful, then, to have a universal language that everyone could understand?

Dr. Zamenhof and His Belief in the Benefits of a Universal Language

2 L. L. Zamenhof believed in such a language. A linguist from Warsaw, Poland, he felt that a common language would contribute to better communication and help ease world tensions. Zamenhof wanted to create a language that did not favor speakers from any geographic area and one that would be easy for everyone to learn. He rejected existing languages because they were either too complicated or would put native speakers at an advantage over others.

3 Zamenhof published his universal language in 1887. It quickly became known as "Esperanto" after his pseudonym, which means "one who is hoping." He was hoping that his language would become accepted and spread throughout the world.

4 Zamenhof did not envision his language as one replacing all other languages but instead as one spoken as a second language by people around the world. In addition to travelers, Esperanto could be useful for anyone wanting to learn more about other cultures. In fact, people from all around the world come together at Esperanto conventions, where the communication barrier is broken because everyone speaks the same language.

An Easy Language to Learn

5 Esperanto is easy to learn. The grammar and other rules of Esperanto are relatively simple, and all words are spelled as they sound. These features make it possible to become fluent in Esperanto much more quickly than in other languages. A knowledge of Esperanto also makes it easier to learn other

California High School Exit Examination

foreign languages, since Esperanto has its roots in many different languages.

6   The majority of the words in Esperanto are derived from Latin and Romance languages, and French in particular. The rest of the vocabulary comes from German, English, Russian, Polish, and Greek. The words were chosen to be as easily recognizable as possible.

7   Most of the letters in Esperanto are pronounced the same way as they are in English. Some of the exceptions are the letter "J," which is pronounced as we would pronounce a "Y," and the letter "R," which is trilled. The letter "G" is always pronounced as in the word "go," and never as in the word "gentle."

8   In Esperanto, it is also easy to identify the different parts of speech. Nouns always end in the letter "o" or "on," with plural nouns ending in "oj" or "ojn." Some common nouns are "amiko" for friend, "libro" for book, and "vorto" for word. Adjectives always end in the letter "a." Some common adjectives in Esperanto are "granda," which means large, and "bruna," which means brown.

9   There are no indefinite articles in Esperanto. The only article used is "la," which is used

like the English word "the." There is no need to learn different articles for masculine or feminine words, or for any cases.

10   Another interesting rule of the language is that word order is more flexible than in most languages. For example, an adjective may be placed before or after a noun.

The Future of Esperanto

11   Although Esperanto is easy to learn, it has not yet achieved widespread usage as a universal language. One reason is that many people simply prefer their own language. They are proud of their country, and their own language is one way to keep that identity.

12   Another reason is that, while many will agree with the idea of a universal language, they do not have the time or motivation to learn one. Learning a new language can be time-consuming, and many people will not take the time to learn one unless they have an inclination to learn languages or see some personal benefit in doing so. Others, perhaps, have not even heard of Esperanto or are unaware that such a universal language exists.

13   Despite Esperanto's seeming lack of popularity, it is estimated that several

million people can speak the language. Many magazines are published in Esperanto, and books—from Shakespeare to Dante— have been translated into Esperanto. Esperanto leagues and organizations help maintain the language and provide interested people with information. Perhaps in the future, Esperanto will find its place as a widely used and accepted universal language.

90B

42. Read this sentence from the passage.

> Learning a new language can be time-consuming, and many people will not take the time to learn one unless they have an inclination to learn languages or see some personal benefit in doing so.

What does the word *inclination* mean?

A liking

B voice

C profit

D indifference

L190B004

43. Based on the passage, which of the following sentences is the BEST conclusion about Zamenhof?

A He wanted the fame that creating a universal language would bring.

B He wanted to make a contribution to world peace and understanding.

C He thought English was the best basis for a universal language.

D He believed that pride in one's country led to conflicts and wars.

L190B006

44. Which of the following sentences BEST summarizes the author's attitude toward Esperanto as expressed in the passage?

A People should be encouraged to learn and speak Esperanto.

B People should learn Esperanto if they are interested in it.

C Esperanto is the perfect language because it is based on many other languages.

D As a universal language, Esperanto has been a huge failure.

L190B015

45. **How does the passage reflect the themes and concerns of the 21st century?**

A   It is about global communication.

B   It describes a particular language.

C   It reinforces the importance of research.

D   It focuses on one person's achievement.

L190B016

The following passage is a rough draft. It may contain errors in grammar, punctuation, sentence structure, and organization. Read the passage and answer questions 46 through 49.

ROUGH DRAFT

My Brain

(1) Sometimes I think I am probably more right-brained, but other times I feel more left-brained. (2) I love to play music and I especially like to make it up as I go along. (3) For anybody else to hear my music, they might think it sounds like noise. (4) My brother, for one, always complains about it.

(5) I also like to write poetry. (6) It is a way for me to put down on paper how I am really feeling. (7) I write things in my poetry I would probably never tell anyone else. (8) I am also pretty good at giving prepared speeches in my English class. (9) Because I really like to do these kinds of things, I feel that I must be right-brained.

(10) But there are other times I am not so sure about it. (11) For example, I am really pretty good at math and other things that require me to be logical. (12) I also think I am pretty good at writing essays about technical things, like explaining how things work. (13) And I'm good at remembering things too.

(14) Though I guess I prefer right-brained activities and can do them more easily, I can do left-brained things pretty well if I have to. (15) I like doing math problems. (16) So I am not sure what that makes me!

012

Practice Test

46. **What is the MOST effective revision of the sentence labeled 3?**

  A For anybody else who hears my music, they might think, sounds like noise.

  B Anybody else might think, hearing my music, that it sounds like noise.

  C Anybody else who hears my music might think it sounds like noise.

  D Leave as is.

  L0012001

47. **What is the BEST way to combine the sentences labeled 12 and 13?**

  A I am good at writing technical essays explaining how things work, and I also have a good memory.

  B Writing technical essays, I am good at explaining how things work and have a good memory.

  C I am good at explaining how things work by writing technical essays and remembering things too.

  D Explaining how things work and technical things are things I am good at writing essays about, and I have a good memory.

  L0012002

48. **Which of the following sentences does NOT fit well in the paragraph in which it is found?**

  A "I love to play music and I especially like to make it up as I go along." (first paragraph)

  B "I also like to write poetry." (second paragraph)

  C "For example, I am really pretty good at math and other things that require me to be logical." (third paragraph)

  D "I like doing math problems." (fourth paragraph)

  L0012003

49. **In which paragraph would the following sentence fit well and improve the essay?**

  Problem solving can be fun for me, and I think crossword puzzles are easy.

  A the first paragraph

  B the second paragraph

  C the third paragraph

  D the fourth paragraph

  L0012004

The following passage is a rough draft. It may contain errors in grammar, punctuation, sentence structure, and organization. Read the passage and answer questions 50 through 51.

ROUGH DRAFT

Water on Mars

(1) For a long time, people have considered the possibility that life may have once existed (or may still exist) on the planet Mars. (2) In 1910, Percival Lowell wrote a book suggesting that a large system of "canals" was built on Mars by a civilization that has since disappeared. (3) The "canals" were grooves on the planet's surface which Lowell saw through a telescope he believed had been built by Martians. (4) We now know that Lowell was wrong—there is no evidence of construction on Mars. (5) However, recent photos from the Mars Orbiter Camera suggest that, until very recently, liquid water flowed on the surface of the planet. (6) And some scientists believe that liquid water might still be found beneath the planet's surface. (7) Why is this important? (8) Well, scientists think that water is necessary for life to develop. (9) If there was (or is) water on Mars, it's quite possible that the planet may have supported life at some point during its history. (10) And if there was once life on Mars, the odds that there is life elsewhere in the Universe become much greater. (11) Scientists warn that it's too early to tell for sure, but maybe we Earthlings are not alone after all.

155

50. **According to the article, which of these facts provides the strongest evidence that life may once have existed on Mars?**

   A   Many people have considered the possibility that life once existed on Mars.

   B   Recent photos suggest that liquid water once flowed on the surface of Mars.

   C   Percival Lowell thought that he saw "canals" on the surface of Mars.

   D   There is no evidence of construction ever having taken place on Mars.

L0155002

51. **What is the correct way to express the ideas in the sentence labeled 3?**

   A   When the "canals" were observed by Lowell, he believed that they had been built by Martians through his telescope.

   B   The "canals" were grooves on the planet's surface that, when observed by Lowell, appeared to have been built by Martians.

   C   Through a telescope, Martians were those who Lowell believed had built the "canals."

   D   Leave as is.

L0155005

California High School Exit Examination

PRACTICE TEST

The following passage is a rough draft. It may contain errors in grammar, punctuation, sentence structure, and organization. Read the passage and answer questions 52 through 55.

ROUGH DRAFT

Essay Writing

(1) To begin an essay, a student should have some knowledge of the topic or be willing to search out information. (2) Then one must focus clearly on the prompt, addressing all its major points, and making sure that the central purpose is evident throughout the entire essay. (3) Interesting and convincing examples with lots of specific details are always helpful. (4) The details must show some kind of clear arrangement—chronological, spatial, or order-of-importance. (5) A student writer will also want to revise a first draft so that any errors in grammar and mechanics can be got rid of. (6) Steps can be taken to edit essays. (7) Relying, solely on "SpellCheck," can be risky; (8) it does not catch the common errors that students make, such as confusing "your" and "you're." (9) If students meet all these requirements, then they will have written very effectively.

198

52. **Which of the following sentences, if inserted before Sentence 1, would make the MOST effective opening sentence?**

    A Writing an essay is easy if one uses a computer.

    B Good essays are always written in black pen.

    C Any student can write a successful essay.

    D Teachers sometimes assign difficult essays.

    L0198001

53. **Sentence 2 would be improved if the word *one* were replaced by—**

    A the writer.

    B you.

    C we.

    D Leave as is.

    L0198003

54. **Which sentence is the MOST effective way of stating the idea in the sentence labeled 7?**

    A One must rely on "SpellCheck" solely.

    B Relying solely on "SpellCheck" can be risky.

    C "SpellCheck" is not always the sole way to check spelling.

    D Leave as is.

    L0198006

55. **Which of the following statements supports the main idea of the essay?**

    A A student should have some knowledge of the topic.

    B Black pens are best for writing essays.

    C One shouldn't just rely on "SpellCheck."

    D One must focus clearly on the prompt, addressing all its major points.

    L0198011

California High School Exit Examination

PRACTICE TEST

The following passage is a rough draft. It may contain errors in grammar, punctuation, sentence structure, and organization. Read the passage and answer questions 56 through 58.

ROUGH DRAFT

Amelia Earhart: An Aviation Pioneer

(1) Earhart began her flying career soon after airplanes were first invented. (2) As a child, she was fascinated by the idea of being a pilot. (3) At the age of 23, she took flying lessons from Neta Snook, one of very few women pilots at the time. (4) In 1921 Earhart bought her own airplane. (5) And she used it to set the first of many aviation records. (6) She flew up to 14,000 feet, setting the women's altitude record.

(7) In 1928 Earhart was the first woman to cross the Atlantic by air. (8) The trip took about 21 hours. (9) She published a book about her experiences and followed it with a lecture tour. (10) A few years later, in 1932, she piloted a plane from Newfoundland to Northern Ireland, making her the first woman to fly across the Atlantic alone. (11) Then she went on to <u>do many other things</u> in aviation. (12) In fact, Earhart became an important pioneer in the world of aviation.

(13) In June of 1937 Earhart and her navigator Frederick Noonan left Miami, Florida, in an attempt to fly around the world. (14) The pair made it to New Guinea on June 30. (15) Earhart and Noonan had traveled a distance of 20,000 miles across the Pacific Ocean before

California High School Exit Examination

PRACTICE TEST

their plane was lost. (16) Amelia Earhart, one of the most renowned aviators in history, dared to attempt the most hazardous flights of her time. (17) In her own words, she summed up her philosophy: "Courage is the price that life exacts for granting peace with yourself."

46B-2

56. Which sentence would BEST begin the essay?

  A This paper is about Amelia Earhart, a famous pilot.

  B Most people like to read about famous pilots.

  C There are several interesting facts about Amelia Earhart, a famous airplane pilot.

  D Amelia Earhart was one of the most famous airplane pilots of her time.

L146B001

58. Which of the following would be the MOST precise way to state the underlined words in the sentence labeled 11?

  A have several other good times

  B take some other actions

  C find other adventures

  D set other records

L146B006

57. What would be the BEST source for information on other records set in the history of aviation?

  A a dictionary of aviation terminology

  B biographies of famous women

  C a world almanac and book of facts

  D a guide to the aircraft industry

L146B004

California High School Exit Examination

PRACTICE TEST

> **For questions 59 through 67, choose the answer that is the most effective substitute for each underlined part of the sentence. If no substitution is necessary, choose "Leave as is."**

59. Responsibilities of the job include <u>greeting customers, escorting them to a table, and offering beverages.</u>

  A greeting customers, escort them to a table and offer a beverage.

  B to greet customers, escorting them to tables and offering a beverage.

  C to greet customers, escorting them to a table, and to offer a beverage.

  D Leave as is.

L00SA041

60. <u>After, the volcano erupted, the</u> tiny tropical island was quiet and devastated.

  A After the volcano erupted, the

  B After the volcano erupted the

  C After the volcano erupts, the

  D Leave as is.

L00SA032

61. <u>If Mark will have made fewer errors, he will have passed his driving test.</u>

  A If Mark would have made fewer errors, he would have passed his driving test.

  B If Mark had made fewer errors, he would have passed his driving test.

  C If Mark would of made fewer errors, he would have passed his driving test.

  D Leave as is.

L00SA037

62. The Alaskan rivers are clear and sparkling <u>in summer however, they are frozen in winter.</u>

  A in summer, however they are frozen in winter.

  B in summer; however, they are frozen in winter.

  C summer: however they are frozen in winter.

  D Leave as is.

L00SA043

63. <u>When the money was stolen by the bandits, the owner</u> of the store felt betrayed.

   A   When the bandits stole the money, the owner

   B   The money was stolen by the bandits. The owner

   C   By the bandits the money was stolen. The owner

   D   Leave as is.

   L00SA026

64. <u>The poetry of Langston Hughes combining the idioms of African-American speech and the rhythms of the blues.</u>

   A   The poetry of Langston Hughes will combine

   B   The poetry of Langston Hughes combines

   C   Langston Hughes' poetry combining

   D   Leave as is.

   L00SA012

65. When our parents celebrate their silver wedding anniversary later this year, <u>they were married for twenty-five years.</u>

   A   they will have been married for twenty-five years.

   B   they have been married for twenty-five years.

   C   they would have been married for twenty-five years.

   D   Leave as is.

   L00SA039

66. <u>"Why should I wear a sweater?"</u> grumbled the boy as his mother reminded him again of the cold weather.

   A   'Why should I wear a sweater'?

   B   "Why should I wear a sweater"

   C   "Why should I wear a sweater"?

   D   Leave as is.

   L00SA201

67. If you want to add your name to the <u>list of volunteers; please</u> go to Room 112.

   A   list of volunteers please;

   B   list of volunteers, please

   C   list of volunteers: please

   D   Leave as is.

   L10SA188

California High School Exit Examination

PRACTICE TEST

> For questions 68 through 72, choose the word or phrase that best completes the sentence.

68. "We should _____ without the captain," the coach said impatiently.

    A proceeds

    B precede

    C precedent

    D proceed

    L00SA020

69. "Which of the three Olympic runners is the _____?" the spectator asked the judge.

    A more fast

    B fastest

    C most fastest

    D most faster

    L00SA023

70. The legendary goddess was the _____ of all the Greek deities.

    A beautifulest

    B more beautiful

    C most beautiful

    D most beautifying

    L00SA022

71. The musician played Wendy's favorite waltz for her husband and _____.

    A I

    B he

    C she

    D her

    L00SA076

72. _____ going to be late if they don't hurry.

    A They're

    B Their

    C There

    D They'll

    L00SA078

California High School Exit Examination

PRACTICE TEST

REMINDER

- ✎ Write your response to the writing prompt below.
- ✎ You may give your writing a title if you would like, but it is not necessary.
- ✎ You may NOT use a dictionary. If you do not know how to spell a word, sound the word out and do the best you can.
- ✎ You may either print or write in cursive.
- ✎ Write clearly! Any erasures or strike-throughs should be as clean as possible.

Writing Task 1:

> In the story "The Hiking Trip," the reader learns about the main character, Jeff. Jeff's personality and emotions are revealed through the actions and dialog presented in the story.
>
> Write an essay in which you describe the personality and emotions of Jeff, the main character. How do his personal characteristics add to the events in the story? How does the author reveal this information about Jeff in the story? Use details and examples from the story to support your ideas.
>
> (10WA2.2)
>
> L0157007

Checklist for Your Writing

The following checklist will help you do your best work. Make sure you:

- ❏ Carefully read the reading passage and the description of the task.
- ❏ Organize your writing with a strong introduction, body, and conclusion.
- ❏ Use specific details and examples from the passage to demonstrate your understanding of the main ideas and the author's purpose.
- ❏ Use precise language that is appropriate for your audience and purpose.
- ❏ Vary your sentences to make your writing interesting to read.
- ❏ Check for mistakes in grammar, spelling, punctuation, capitalization, and sentence formation.

NOTE: The CAHSEE Response to Literature Scoring Guide for this writing task may be found on page 115. "The Hiking Trip" is on page 103.

California High School Exit Examination

PRACTICE TEST

 **REMINDER**

- Write your response to the writing prompt below.
- You may give your writing a title if you would like, but it is not necessary.
- You may NOT use a dictionary. If you do not know how to spell a word, sound the word out and do the best you can.
- You may either print or write in cursive.
- Write clearly! Any erasures or strike-throughs should be as clean as possible.

Writing Task 2:

> By the time students enter high school, they have learned about many moments in history that have influenced our world today. Think about a moment in history you studied and consider its importance.
>
> Write a composition in which you discuss a moment in history. Share its importance in today's world. Be sure to support the moment with details and examples.
>
> (10WA2.3)   L0000064

Checklist for Your Writing

The following checklist will help you do your best work. Make sure you:

- ❏ Read the description of the task carefully.
- ❏ Use specific details and examples to fully support your ideas.
- ❏ Organize your writing with a strong introduction, body, and conclusion.
- ❏ Choose specific words that are appropriate for your audience and purpose.
- ❏ Vary your sentences to make your writing interesting to read.
- ❏ Check for mistakes in grammar, spelling, punctuation, and sentence formation.

NOTE: The CAHSEE Response to Writing Prompt Scoring Guide for this task may be found on page 117.

Practice Test

California High School Exit Examination

PRACTICE TEST

 REMINDER

- ✎ Write your response to the writing prompt below.
- ✎ You may give your writing a title if you would like, but it is not necessary.
- ✎ You may NOT use a dictionary. If you do not know how to spell a word, sound the word out and do the best you can.
- ✎ You may either print or write in cursive.
- ✎ Write clearly! Any erasures or strike-throughs should be as clean as possible.

Writing Task 3:

> Some students at your school expressed an interest in making the school more attractive by getting rid of the trash on the school grounds.
>
> Write a persuasive essay for your school paper in which you convince the readers of the importance of getting rid of the trash and making the school more attractive. Convince your readers through the use of specific reasons and examples.
>
> (10WA2.4)
>
> L0000060

Checklist for Your Writing

The following checklist will help you do your best work. Make sure you:

- ❏ Read the description of the task carefully.
- ❏ Organize your writing with a strong introduction, body, and conclusion.
- ❏ State your position, support it with specific examples, and address the reader's concerns.
- ❏ Use words that are appropriate for your audience and purpose.
- ❏ Vary your sentences to make your writing interesting to read.
- ❏ Check for mistakes in grammar, spelling, punctuation, capitalization, and sentence formation.

NOTE: The CAHSEE Response to Writing Prompt Scoring Guide for this writing task may be found on page 117.

OVERVIEW OF THE STANDARDS

In six broad categories, the State of California defines what 10th Graders should know about English-language arts. These are the formal descriptions of those six categories and the number of test questions from each category that appear on the CAHSEE.

❑ **Word Analysis** **Students apply their knowledge of word origins to determine the meaning of new words encountered in reading materials and to use those words accurately.** **(7 multiple-choice questions)**
❑ **Reading Comprehension** **Students read and understand a wide variety of classic and contemporary literature, magazines, newspapers, and online information. Students analyze the organizational patterns, arguments, and positions advanced. (18 multiple-choice questions)**
❑ **Literary Response and Analysis** **Students read and respond to historically or culturally significant works of literature that reflect and enhance their studies of history and social science. Students conduct in-depth analyses of recurrent patterns and themes. (20 multiple-choice questions)**
❑ **Writing Strategies** **Students write clear, coherent, and focused essays. The writing exhibits students' awareness of audience and purpose. Essays contain formal introductions, supporting evidence, and conclusions. (12 multiple-choice questions)**
❑ **Writing Conventions** **Students write and speak with a command of standard English language conventions including grammar, sentence construction, and paragraph structure.** **(15 multiple-choice questions)**
❑ **Writing Applications** **Students write one essay. The essay will be a response to one of the following: a literary or expository passage, a biographical narrative, a persuasive essay, or a business letter.** **(1 essay)**

These are the categories that will appear on your student score report. In greater detail, these broad categories are defined by "standards." The CAHSEE measures 33 standards. The following pages describe those standards, the types of test questions that measure the standards, and more strategies you can use to pass the CAHSEE.

Word Analysis, Fluency, and Systematic Vocabulary Development

7 questions	18 questions	20 questions	12 questions	15 questions	1 question
Word Analysis, Fluency, and Systematic Vocabulary Development	Reading Comprehension	Literary Response and Analysis	Writing Strategies	Written and Oral English Language Conventions	Writing Applications

These are the 2 CAHSEE Word Analysis Standards.

The CAHSEE uses 7 multiple-choice questions to measure these standards. There is no magic list of words that will appear on the test, so this section of the Study Guide discusses some of the strategies that can help you succeed.

You will be asked to explain what a particular word or phrase means. The CAHSEE measures your understanding of both denotation (the dictionary definition) and connotation (the image or feeling that a word or phrase suggests to readers). For example, *house* and *home* have the same denotation: both describe a place of shelter. However, their connotations are quite different. *House* makes most readers think of particular buildings where people live; *home* suggests warmth, comfort, and safety.

If you are not already familiar with a word or phrase in a test question, you will need to apply skills and strategies such as gathering meaning from context or using your knowledge of word origins, roots, prefixes, and suffixes.

These passages and questions are from a previous version of the CAHSEE. Read each passage and answer each question. After each question, a strategy is provided to help you practice your word analysis skills.

10RW1.1 Identify and use the literal and figurative meanings of words and understand word derivations. [5 questions]

10RW1.2 Distinguish between the denotative and connotative meanings of words and interpret the connotative power of words. [2 questions]

Read this passage from a previous CAHSEE administration and the discussion and question that follow.

The Piano Lesson

1 I walked up the front stoop to the porch of Mrs. Windsor's house and waited outside as I always did when I heard the piano. That meant she was working with another student, and I was not supposed to disturb them by ringing the bell. I leaned against the rough brick exterior and daydreamed about what I'd rather be doing. "Almost anything," I sighed dejectedly. I had been tutored enough to read, understand, and even write some musical compositions, but I just didn't have a flair for it. It didn't come to me naturally. I thought back to happier times when I was writing stories and acting them out with my friends, cutting up old clothes and rags to make costumes, and building props and scenery out of old junk we found. But Mrs. Windsor had offered to give me the lessons for free, so I felt obligated to try.

2 The door opened and Wendy Barton stood there with her sheet music tucked under her arm. She wrinkled her nose at me and whisked by. I guess she thought mediocre piano playing might be contagious.

3 I walked into Mrs. Windsor's music room, sat down on the piano bench, and began to sort through my sheet music.

4 "Hello," I heard a voice behind me say softly. I turned around to see a petite girl standing behind me, eating an apple.

5 "Want one?" she offered.

6 "No, thanks, I don't want to get the keys all sticky. Mrs. Windsor wouldn't like that." I pointed to the polished piano in front of me. "But thanks, anyway."

7 "What's your name?" she asked.

8 But before I could answer, Mrs. Windsor bustled into the room in her usual urgent manner and announced, "Jennifer, this is my niece, Pasha. Pasha, this is Jennifer. Pasha will be giving you your lesson today. I'm up to my ears in plumbers! There will be no charge, as usual, just good practice." Her voice trailed off as she exited to the kitchen.

9 Pasha set her apple down on the side table and slid beside me on the piano bench.

10 "What piece do you like the best?" she inquired.

11 "What do you mean?" I asked. "They're all the same to me. I don't know."

12 "You mean you don't have a favorite?"

13 "No, not really."

14 Pasha looked at me, rather puzzled, then opened my sheet music to the beginning page and asked me to play. I arranged my fingers on the keys and studied the notes on the page for a moment. Then I furrowed my brow and concentrated to make the notes on the page match the finger movements. I have to admit I was a rather mechanical pianist.

15 After about a page or two, Pasha gently put her hand on top of mine as if to hush my fingers. There was a long pause. "Jennifer, what are you hearing in the music?"

16 I looked at her rather strangely and admitted I didn't know what she meant.

17 "Like a story. What story is being played out within the music?"

18 "I guess I've never thought about it before. I don't know."

19 "Here, let me try and you listen," Pasha instructed.

20 She closed her eyes and took a deep breath, letting her fingers dangle lightly over the keys. Then, she began to play. "See, it begins here beside some kind of river or brook. Hear the water trickling beside you?"

21 Her fingers rippled over some high melodic chain of chords. "Now the princess appears and she's picking flowers from the water's edge." A carefree, happy tune filled the air in time to Pasha's dancing fingers. "Oh, but she slips!" The music changed. "And our princess is being carried off by the roaring current. Quickly, the princess's horse sees her plight," Pasha continued dramatically, "and races to the river's edge where he swims out to let her catch hold of his halter. They make it to the bank and she hugs her faithful horse and swears she will never again wear princess skirts of billowing layers and petticoats that weigh her down. She will only wear jeans and T-shirts from now on." Pasha finished with a flourish and a mischievous grin and then looked at me.

22 "Aren't you the girl who tells the stories?" she asked.

23 "I guess. I do tell a lot of stories."

24 "Oh, yes! All the kids talk about them. I've heard about you."

25 "Well, all you have to do is learn to hear the stories in the music. That's all there is to it."

26 "I've never thought of it that way."

27 "Let's try another one, shall we?" Pasha smiled and together we played that afternoon, finding the story in the music and learning that sometimes it takes a friend to pull you out of the river onto dry land again.

L140B007

Sample CAHSEE question
Read this sentence from paragraph 14 of the passage.

> I have to admit I was a rather
> mechanical pianist.

The author's use of the word *mechanical* suggests that Jennifer played the piano without—

A sheet music.

B proper practice.

C emotion.

D help.

Strategy

Be sure to read the question carefully. Paragraph 14 establishes that Jennifer *does* use sheet music, and proper practice and help are *not* the topics of this paragraph. Even if you did not know what "mechanical" implies, you have arrived at the correct answer by eliminating wrong options. This strategy will help you with many questions you encounter in the CAHSEE.

Read this passage from a previous CAHSEE administration and the discussion and question that follow.

Papier-Mâché Mobile Galaxy

This fun mobile is easy and economical to make; it adds color to any room. You can create many variations, depending on the colors of paper and the sizes of the balloons. You can name your "galaxy" any name you wish! Preparation: Place newspapers in your work area to catch drips of paste and make cleanup easy.

Materials needed:

six balloons	paintbrush
an empty jelly jar	floral wire (available at craft stores)
wheat paste (available at craft stores)	coat hanger
colored tissue paper or crêpe paper streamers	string, about 3 feet in length
scissors	clothespins

Instructions:

1. Blow up each balloon to the size you desire. Vary the sizes to make the mobile more interesting. Rest each balloon on the empty jar when you are ready to work on it.

2. Cut or tear the tissue paper or crêpe paper streamers into strips. Brush a small amount of wheat paste on the balloon. Apply the tissue paper, working vertically from the top of the balloon down toward the knot. Brush on a little more paste, and add another strip of paper, slightly overlapping the first. Continue to apply the strips of paper until the entire balloon is covered. Then add additional layers of paper. You will need about four layers of paper to ensure the stability of the ball.

3. Stretch the string between two chairs. Hang the paper-covered balloons on the string by the knot, using the clothespins. Drying will take several hours. After the paper is dry, hold the knot of the balloon and use the scissors to pop the balloon and remove the knot.

4. Cut six lengths of floral wire, varying the lengths between 6 inches and 12 inches. Thread about 1 ½ inches of the wire through the end of the ball opposite the opening for the balloon knot. Twist the end of the wire around itself to secure it. Attach the other end of the wire to the coat hanger, arranging each ball across the wire to achieve the effect desired.

5. Hang the mobile wherever you wish. It can brighten any part of a room, especially if hung near a sunny window. There the light can reflect off the colors.

31B

L131B002

Sample CAHSEE question
Read this sentence from the instructions.

You can create many variations,
depending on the colors of paper
and the sizes of the balloons.

The word *variations* is based on the word vary, which means—

A choose.

B decide.

C change.

D build.

Strategy

Be sure to look for context clues. The instructions include a description of the possible product "…depending on the colors of paper and sizes of the balloons." Obviously the mobile's appearance depends on which color of paper and size of balloon one chooses.

For more practice on these types of questions, go to the Released Test Questions at http://www.cde.ca.gov/ta/tg/hs/resources.asp.

Reading Comprehension

Word Analysis, Fluency, and Systematic Vocabulary Development	Reading Comprehension	Literary Response and Analysis	Writing Strategies	Written and Oral English Language Conventions	Writing Applications

These are the 6 CAHSEE Reading Comprehension Standards.

The CAHSEE uses 18 multiple-choice questions to measure these standards. Reading comprehension involves several skills, so this section of the Study Guide provides strategies to help you succeed.

You will be asked to read and understand informational documents such as textbooks, instruction manuals, articles, and letters. The test questions, all multiple choice, ask you to connect the information to related concepts and identify main ideas, supporting details, text organization, logic, and author's purpose.

These passages and questions are from a previous version of the CAHSEE. Read each passage and answer each question. After each question, a strategy is provided to help you understand and practice your reading comprehension skills.

8RC2.1 Compare and contrast the features and elements of consumer materials to gain meaning from documents (e.g., warranties, contracts, product information, instruction manuals). [1 question]

10RC2.1 Analyze the structure and format of functional workplace documents, including the graphics and headers, and explain how authors use the features to achieve their purposes. [3 questions]

10RC2.4 Synthesize the content from several sources or works by a single author dealing with a single issue; paraphrase the ideas and connect them to other sources and related topics to demonstrate comprehension. [3 questions]

10RC2.5 Extend ideas presented in primary or secondary sources through original analysis, evaluation, and elaboration. [3 questions]

10RC2.7 Critique the logic of functional documents by examining the sequence of information and procedures in anticipation of possible reader misunderstandings. [3 questions]

10RC2.8 Evaluate the credibility of an author's argument or defense of a claim by critiquing the relationship between generalizations and evidence, the comprehensiveness of evidence, and the way in which the author's intent affects the structure and tone of the text (e.g., in professional journals, editorials, political speeches, primary source material). [5 questions]

Read this passage from a previous CAHSEE administration and the discussion and questions that follow.

Slow Death of a Cave

An onslaught of tourists threatens the pristine grandeur of Kartchner Caverns

By Leslie Vreeland

1 One by one, the brown-eared bats squeeze through a six-inch hole and emerge into deepening twilight; an instant later, they have fluttered off to feed. At Kartchner Caverns, flocks of bats have repeated this ritual each summer evening for 40,000 years. But these days, with the advent of tourism, the bats are not the only creatures shuttling in and out of this labyrinthine world of darkness. Since Kartchner was opened to the public two years ago, tours have been selling out weeks in advance. So far the bats still appear to be thriving. But the cave itself may be dying.

2 Located just 30 miles north of the Mexican border in southern Arizona's austere Whetstone Mountains, Kartchner is a pristine example of a living cave, with formations that are still moist and growing. The brilliant orange, red, and gold stalactites and stalagmites in the caverns have been formed and fed during the past 200,000 years by rainwater that combines with carbon dioxide from the air and carbon from the soil, trickles through limestone, and finally seeps through the earth to deposit mineral-laden droplets.

3 The state of Arizona recently spent 12 years and $30 million to turn this subterranean fairyland of spires, turrets, and shields into what officials have dubbed the Environmental Cave, taking pains to protect it from the potential damage caused by tourism.

4 Kartchner's formations depend on moisture, so humidity must be maintained at 99 percent or the fantastic structures will stop growing. A temperature variant of just half a degree can dry out the cave within weeks. But there's a scalding desert above and 500 tourists come through each day, so visitors must enter through two steel doors designed to keep hot air from seeping in. Misters spray the cave floor to keep it damp.

5 Visitors are treated to an impressive, if garish, display: At the end of the tour, in front of the grandest formation of all, the cave suddenly goes dark, New Age music swells, and dozens of pulsating lasers swirl about the towering Kubla Khan, a 58-foot-high column of sandstone. And that is part of the problem. The high intensity of the lights, say cave specialists, can cause algae to grow on the formations and dull them. The humidifying misters may be causing additional damage by disturbing airflow patterns, air temperature, and mineral deposits, and by disrupting the delicate ecosystem supporting the cave's various

life-forms. Despite protests from scientists, the misters now run around the clock—not 12 hours a day, as originally planned—to compensate for the unexpected impact of tourists. Yet, the cave is still drying out. One year after Kartchner opened, it was less humid and one degree warmer in areas where the public visits. (Despite several requests, officials failed to provide new data.)

6   Park officials have suggested that the cave is dry because of a recent drought and note that hard rains have since fallen and added moisture. Nevertheless, they have hired a paleontologist to assess the impact of tourism on the cave and to devise new ways to avert further damage. Ronal Kerbo, the National Park Service's leading expert on cave preservation, remains optimistic but warns, "Kartchner will never be a pristine environment again. This is what happens when you open a cave to the public and say, 'Come on in.'"

From *Discover*, November 2001. Copyright © 2001, Leslie Vreeland. Used by permission of the author.

21C

L121C009

Sample CAHSEE question
Based on information in the last paragraph of the passage, it is likely that in the future—

A the public will return Kartchner to its original condition.

B changes will be made to save Kartchner from further damage.

C the state of Arizona will close Kartchner to the public.

D other caves will be found near the Kartchner site.

Strategy
It is important to read the question carefully. Notice that it directs the reader to the *last* paragraph of the passage. The final sentence of the passage denies one of the options and the final paragraph admits that the cave is open to the public with *no* suggestion of possibly closing the cave. Another of the options is *not* discussed at all in the final paragraph. The correct answer should be easy to identify if you take your time and look for which option is the subject of the final paragraph.

L121C010

Sample CAHSEE question
What information from the passage supports the idea that the temperature plays an important role in the life of cave formations?

A . . . brilliant orange, red, and gold stalactites and stalagmites in the caverns have been formed . . .

B . . . visitors must enter through two steel doors designed to keep hot air from seeping in.

C . . . hard rains have since fallen and added moisture.

D . . . they have hired a paleontologist to assess the impact of tourism on the cave . . .

Strategy
Look for the *only* option that makes any reference to temperature – "…hot air…." Therefore, it is easy to eliminate the other options.

Sample CAHSEE question
Which statement can BEST be supported with information from the passage?

A Measures taken to protect Kartchner Caverns have not been totally successful.

B Visitors to Kartchner Caverns are from many other states and countries around the world.

C If Kartchner Caverns were to die, tourists would no longer want to visit there.

D Kartchner Caverns is very different from other caverns around the world.

Strategy
Be sure to read questions carefully. Although all four options might be possibilities, the question asks which is the *best* option. Some are *not* supported by the passage. The majority of the passage discusses experiments that do not always produce the desired results, such as unintentionally adding algae to "Kubla Khan" or changing airflow patterns by using humidifying misters.

Sample CAHSEE question
The passage provides the MOST information on the—

A causes of damage to Kartchner Caverns.

B location of Kartchner Caverns.

C inhabitants of Kartchner Caverns.

D age of Kartchner Caverns.

Strategy
Be sure to read questions carefully. Some facts in the options are only mentioned once in the passage. However, *most* of the passage discusses the causes of damage to the cave such as changes in temperature, moisture, lighting, and the effects of tourists.

L121C017

Sample CAHSEE question
Which of the following BEST represents the opposing forces present in this passage?

A   society versus progress

B   society versus nature

C   politics versus society

D   politics versus industry

Strategy

Caves are phenomena of nature. Look for the option referring to nature. Also, the passage discusses trying to balance the cave's delicate environment with the effects of people, "society," entering the cave. Lastly, always pay attention to emphasis words such as "best."

Read this passage from a previous CAHSEE administration and the discussion and questions that follow.

The Cellular Phone

PRODUCT DESCRIPTION

This simple to use yet powerful cell phone will help you stay connected with family and friends—no matter the time, no matter the situation, no matter the location. Getting the most out of your wireless device couldn't be easier as long as you follow these basic instructions.

EFFICIENT AND SAFE PHONE OPERATION

1. Always be courteous to others when using your phone. If possible, move to a secluded location when using your phone.
2. Remember to mute the ring tone (see instructions) when you are in the company of others who do not wish to be disturbed.
3. Speak with your normal volume when the phone is in use.
4. Do not use the phone while driving.
5. Turn the phone off in health care facilities.

BASIC OPERATION

Turning the Phone On and Off

Press and hold ON/OFF until the phone beeps. The display window beneath the product logo and the keypad backlighting come on for about 15 seconds. To turn the phone off, press and hold ON/OFF until the phone beeps and the display goes blank.

Placing a Call

To place a call, the phone must be ON, and a system name must be present in the display window (*Home 1*, for example).

1. Enter the phone number by pressing the number keys. The numbers will appear in the display. If you enter a wrong number, briefly press CLR (clear) to erase it. Press and hold CLR to erase all digits you have entered.
2. Press YES. The word *Dialing* will appear in the display while the phone attempts to access the cellular system. When the phone accesses the cellular system, *In Use* replaces the system name in the display window, and *Call* replaces *Dialing*.
3. When the call is finished, press ON/OFF to end the call.

Answering a Call

When a call is received, the ring tone sounds. Then the message *Call Receive* flashes in the display; the display and the keypad backlighting flash; and the indicator light on top of the phone rapidly flashes green.

1. Press YES to answer the call. The words *Call Receive* are replaced by the call timer, and the words *In Use* are shown in the bottom line of the display.

2. Press and hold ON/OFF to end the call.

Muting the Ring Tone

To mute the ring tone without answering the call, press ON/OFF. *Call Receive* is still shown in the display window. You can still answer the call by pressing YES.

Making Emergency Calls

The phone was programmed with an emergency number (911) when it was manufactured. The programmed emergency number can be dialed and called at any time, regardless of any call restrictions you have set through the LOCKS menu.

DISPLAY MESSAGES

The following are messages typically seen on the display window of the phone:

Home 1

Cellular service is coming from your home service. The number (1 – 4) at the end of the message indicates the phone number you are using.

Roam

Cellular service is coming from a system other than the home system. The letter A or B is also shown with the Roam message to indicate if the roaming system is a type A or a type B cellular system.

Privacy

The cellular service is coming from a private system.

Call Receive

The phone is receiving a call.

Dialing

The phone is dialing the number shown in the display.

In Use

The phone has a call active.

206

Sample CAHSEE question
Which of the following is covered by this manual?

A   operating instructions for cell phone users

B   the history and inventor of the cell phone

C   buying additional cell phone accessories

D   installing additional cell phone buttons

Strategy

This type of question is easiest to answer if you eliminate all the topics that are *not* discussed in a passage. Look for the overall purpose of the entire passage.

Sample CAHSEE question
Under which heading would one look to find information on how to mute the phone's ring?

A   Product Description

B   Efficient and Safe Phone Operation

C   Basic Operation

D   Display Messages

Strategy

Keep in mind that the question is asking how to use a product, in this case, how to mute the phone's ring. An option describing a product is not the same as telling how to use a product. Although one option does refer to "operation," a careful reading shows that the option includes "safe" operation. This option goes beyond what the question is asking. Another option does not pertain to how to use the product. No doubt you were able to identify the correct answer.

L0206004

Sample CAHSEE question
What is the correct order for the steps to place a call with the digital phone?

1 Press NO/ON/OFF to end call.

2 Enter phone number by pressing numeric keys.

3 Press NO/ON/OFF until phone beeps.

4 When digits appear, press yes.

A 1, 3, 4, 2

B 3, 2, 4, 1

C 4, 3, 2, 1

D 2, 4, 1, 3

Strategy

In order to place a phone call, the first step should always be turning on the cell phone. Notice that there is only one option that begins with this first, most important step.

L0206005

Sample CAHSEE question
What should one do before entering a phone number?

A Lay the phone down.

B Turn the phone to mute.

C Turn the phone on.

D Activate the display window.

Strategy
Be sure you understand the proper sequence of steps in a process.
The correct answer has to state the most essential first step.

L0206006

Sample CAHSEE question
What does the message *Roam* indicate?

A You must dial the number again.

B You have an incoming call.

C You are not using your home system service.

D You may not use the phone at this time.

Strategy
This type of question requires you to go back to the passage. In this
case you will notice that the "Roam" section of the passage includes
the phrase "…other than the home system." This is very similar to
the wording of one of the options.

Let's move on to the Literary Response and Analysis Strand.
For more practice on these types of questions, go to the Released
Test Questions at http://www.cde.ca.gov/ta/tg/hs/resources.asp.

7 questions	18 questions	20 questions	12 questions	15 questions	1 question
Word Analysis, Fluency, and Systematic Vocabulary Development	**Reading Comprehension**	**Literary Response and Analysis**	**Writing Strategies**	**Written and Oral English Language Conventions**	**Writing Applications**

These are the 12 CAHSEE Literary Response and Analysis Standards.

There are 20 multiple-choice questions that measure these standards. Literary response and analysis involves several skills, so this section of the Study Guide discusses some strategies that can help you succeed.

You will be asked to read and understand stories, poems, plays, and essays. You should also be familiar with common literary devices and figurative language, especially the types found in poetry. The passages often deal with themes also present in other subjects such as social studies. The test questions, all multiple-choice, ask you to identify character traits, conflicts and relationships, and analyze patterns and themes.

These passages and questions are from a previous version of the CAHSEE. Read each passage and answer each question. After each question, a strategy is provided to help you understand and practice your literary response and analysis skills.

10RL3.1 Articulate the relationship between the expressed purposes and the characteristics of different forms of dramatic literature (e.g., comedy, tragedy, drama, dramatic monologue). [2 questions]

10RL3.3 Analyze interactions between main and subordinate characters in a literary text (e.g., internal and external conflicts, motivations, relationships, influences) and explain the way those interactions affect the plot. [2 questions]

10RL3.4 Determine characters' traits by what the characters say about themselves in narration, dialogue, dramatic monologue, and soliloquy. [2 questions]

10RL3.5 Compare works that express a universal theme and provide evidence to support the ideas expressed in each work. [2 questions]

10RL3.6 Analyze and trace an author's development of time and sequence, including the use of complex literary devices (e.g., foreshadowing, flashbacks). [2 questions]

10RL3.7 Recognize and understand the significance of various literary devices, including figurative language, imagery, allegory, and symbolism, and explain their appeal. [2 questions]

10RL3.8 Interpret and evaluate the impact of ambiguities, subtleties, contradictions, ironies, and incongruities in a text. [2 questions]

10RL3.9 Explain how voice, persona, and the choice of a narrator affect characterization and the tone, plot, and credibility of a text. [2 questions]

10RL3.10 Identify and describe the function of dialogue, scene designs, soliloquies, asides, and character foils in dramatic literature. [1 question]

8RL.3.7 Analyze a work of literature, showing how it reflects the heritage, traditions, attitudes, and beliefs of its author. (Biographical approach) [Standards 8RL3.7 or 10RL3.11 or 10RL3.12 will be rotated for a total of 3 questions per test form.]

10RL3.11 Evaluate the aesthetic qualities of style, including the impact of diction and figurative language, on tone, mood, and theme, using the terminology of literary criticism. (Aesthetic approach) [Standards 8RL3.7 or 10RL3.11 or 10RL3.12 will be rotated for a total of 3 questions per test form.]

10RL3.12 Analyze the way in which a work of literature is related to the themes and issues of its historical period. (Historical approach) [Standards 8RL3.7 or 10RL3.11 or 10RL3.12 will be rotated for a total of 3 questions per test form.]

Read this passage from a previous CAHSEE administration and the discussion and questions that follow.

The Pendulum Swings

1   Of all the days to forget to set the alarm! Running to catch the bus and trying to gather everything she needed for school had left her feeling very frazzled. Sheri felt rushed as she began her science test.

2   As Sheri left the room, a pounding headache reminded her that she was certain that the test had not gone well. How could it have? Not a moment all morning to relax. No time to review. No time to remind herself how well prepared she was. All because she forgot to set her clock for the first time since she had started attending school! "No one to blame but myself," she lamented.

3   That afternoon, she left school to go to work. She had been working at Beckman's for two years, three afternoons a week. Finishing up for the night, Mrs. Beckman called her into the main office. "Sheri," she said, "you have been a great worker, and we really appreciate all that you have done, but business has been slow. We have to let you go. I'll happily give you a recommendation for another job."

4   Sheri was shocked. She left the office in a daze. As she walked slowly towards her aunt's house, Sheri tried to think about the new hair style her aunt had promised her. When she arrived at the house, Sheri handed her aunt the magazine clipping that showed the cut and color she wanted, leaned back in the chair, and relaxed for the first time all day.

5   "Well, you're done. What do you think?" her aunt asked about an hour later.

6   Sheri slowly rotated her chair towards the mirror, very excited. What she saw left her speechless. It was absolutely nothing like the picture! How could she possibly go to school again? She thanked her aunt and left, feeling dejected.

7   The next day, she arrived at school early. She had set her alarm to make sure that she didn't repeat her experience of the day before. Putting her things in her locker, she was approached by Ms. Drobick, the teacher who had given the test the day before.

8 "I know, Ms. Drobick, I did very poorly on the test. It's just that I forgot . . ."

9 "What are you talking about? Sheri, you did a great job! Best score I've ever seen!"
Ms. Drobick said. "What I wanted to ask you is if you would be interested in working
a few days a week after school as a lab assistant. I need some help organizing and labeling
all the materials."

10 Sheri accepted. Not only would it be more interesting than working at Beckman's, but she
would also earn more money!

11 "Sheri!" she heard as the rest of the students began to enter the building. "Where did you
get your hair done?" She was so happy about her test and new job that she had momentarily
forgotten about her hair. She was instantly mortified.

12 "Wow! You look amazing! That is soooo cool!" she was told. She couldn't believe her ears.
Everyone absolutely loved her hair!

13 What a couple of days it had been! Walking home, she smiled as the radio of a passing car
blared the song "What a Difference a Day Makes!"

03C

L103C001

Sample CAHSEE question
This passage is an example of what literary genre?

A fiction

B drama

C essay

D autobiography

Strategy
Make sure that you know the characteristics of various literary genres. Dramas are always written in the form of plays with a list of characters, the setting, and identifications of each speaker. Essays are short compositions on a particular subject or theme. Autobiographies are accounts of a person's life told by that person. This passage tells a story, most likely a made-up story. Even though what is being told might happen in real life, the passage mainly intends to entertain by telling a story.

L103C004

Sample CAHSEE question
Which sentence BEST states the main theme of the passage?

A Life is full of uncertainty.

B Things are not always as bad as they seem.

C Time lost is never found.

D True happiness is not found in material things.

Strategy
Make sure you understand what the question is asking. The question asks about theme. Think of plot as *what* happens, and think of theme as *why* the author is making certain events happen. What is the point the author is trying to make? The theme is a dominant idea running throughout a passage. Also, pay attention to key words such as *best*. Although all four options are themes, some options do not pertain to the passage. In the passage, all these "disasters" turned out well, pointing to only one clear correct answer.

Read this passage from a previous CAHSEE administration and the discussion and questions that follow.

The School Garden

Cast:

MR. EMERSON, teacher

Students in his class

(*Setting: Desert Sky High School, MR. EMERSON's English class*)

MR. EMERSON: (*As he finishes taking attendance.*) Vargas, Warner, and Zuniga. Everyone's here today. That's great, because I have good news! Remember that "Keep America Beautiful" essay contest we entered a few weeks ago that was sponsored by Lakeside Nursery?

(*Class murmurs, acknowledging this.*)

MR. EMERSON: We had an entry that came in first place. Raymond won with his essay on recycling! According to the judges, you *all* did very well, and they said it was a tough contest to judge. I'm really proud of you all!

SARAH: So, Mr. Emerson, what exactly did Raymond win?

MR. EMERSON: Well, since it was someone from *our* class, we will be able to select plants from Lakeside Nursery and plant them on the school grounds.

(*The class groans.*)

SARAH: *That's* the prize? Plants for the school?

MR. EMERSON: Hey! Think about it. This will be great. We can find a little spot on the school grounds, fix it up with some colorful plants, and we can go there on nice afternoons and read or write in our journals. Plus, it will make the school look nicer. Everyone will enjoy it.

NATHAN: So, you're saying that we can attend class *outside*?

MR. EMERSON: Sure! I think it would be nice to hold class outdoors now and then.

(*Class begins to show approval.*)

HECTOR: Way to go, Raymond!

RENE: Yeah, I could use some fresh air about this time of day.

ALEX: So could I. But I had some place in mind other than the school grounds. Maybe the skate park!

MR. EMERSON: (*Laughing.*) Sorry, not an option, Alex. We're talking about creating a garden, which brings me to my next question: What kind of garden would you like to create?

JEN: A rose garden.

MR. EMERSON: Rose gardens are nice. Yes, Carolina?

CAROLINA: Last week in Mrs. Villareal's biology class we had a botanist come as a guest speaker.

KARL: A whatanist?

CAROLINA: A botanist. A scientist who studies plants. Anyway, she said that Xeriscaping™[1] is a smart way to garden in this desert area.

KARL: Now you're *really* confusing me! What's Xeriscaping?

MAX: Oh, I know! In our area, that's when you use indigenous plants in your garden.

KARL: (*Rolling his eyes.*) Why is it that people always use a complicated word when they're defining another complicated word?

MR. EMERSON: Can anyone help Karl and tell him what indigenous means?

MACY: (*Thumbing through her dictionary.*) It says here: "existing, growing, or produced naturally in a region or country."

MR. EMERSON: Good job, Macy! That's a dictionary point for you. (*Addressing class.*) Why do you think it's a smart way to garden? (*Pauses.*) Yes, Jennifer?

JENNIFER: Well, I think indigenous plants would require less watering, and that would save the school time and money.

MR. EMERSON: Good point. In fact, Xeriscaping means growing plants with little water. Anything else?

JAMAL: If it grows in this region anyway, then it probably would be something that would be compatible with the soil, right?

MR. EMERSON: Makes sense. Anyone else?

JESSIE: It would probably need less maintenance than something that grows in another region.

MR. EMERSON: Very good! I like the idea of Xeriscaping, but I'm also open for other ideas. Anyone?

(*No one responds.*)

MR. EMERSON: Okay, then give me a show of hands. Who wants to have a Xeriscape garden?

(*Most of the students raise their hands.*)

MR. EMERSON: Okay then, a Xeriscape garden it is. (*Looks at the clock on the wall.*) Now, with the time we have left, why don't we go outside and find a spot for our new garden?

(*The class exits excitedly.*)

---

[1] Pronounced ZER-i-scaping

03A

Literary Response

L103A003

Sample CAHSEE question
Where does the drama take place?

A in an auditorium

B in a skate park

C outside a school building

D in a classroom

Strategy
Remember that in a drama, directly below the list of characters is the setting. Questions that ask where the action takes place are asking about setting. To answer this question correctly, you only need to look back at the beginning of the drama.

L103A004

Sample CAHSEE question
How does the students' attitude about the garden change during the play?

A from hopeful to disappointed

B from unenthusiastic to supportive

C from worried to confident

D from approving to disapproving

Strategy
You can easily eliminate options that end in negative adjectives because the stage instructions tell that at the end of the play "the class exits excitedly." You know that the students were not worried about winning the plants; they just were not excited at first. By eliminating incorrect options, you can find the correct answer.

For more practice on these types of questions, go to the Released Test Questions at http://www.cde.ca.gov/ta/tg/hs/resources.asp.

In the last three chapters, we have addressed the differences between fiction, biography, articles, and essays; asked you to read selections carefully for context clues, details, and evidence; encouraged you to use your common sense; given you some techniques for figuring out theme and main idea; and discussed tone.

One more tip. Reading—reading every day—will help you become a better reader. Reading and discussing what you read will help even more.

Writing Strategies

7 questions	18 questions	20 questions	12 questions	15 questions	1 question
Word Analysis, Fluency, and Systematic Vocabulary Development	Reading Comprehension	Literary Response and Analysis	Writing Strategies	Written and Oral English Language Conventions	Writing Applications

These are the 5 CAHSEE Writing Strategies Standards.

The CAHSEE uses 12 multiple-choice questions to test these standards. In this section, you do not write any essays, but you answer questions about writing. Most of the questions ask you to find and correct errors, and choose better words and phrases. You should be able to recognize clear, logical writing. You must identify purpose, audience, organization, and supporting details. Also, you will be expected to evaluate various research sources. See how you do on the ten questions in this chapter.

If you know some effective writing strategies, you can improve your own writing. You also can help your classmates improve their writing when you work in pairs and do peer responses.

These passages and questions are from a previous version of the CAHSEE. Read each passage and answer each question. After each question, a solution is provided to help you understand and practice your writing strategies skills.

10WS1.1 Establish a controlling impression or coherent thesis that conveys a clear and distinctive perspective on the subject and maintain a consistent tone and focus throughout the piece of writing. [3 questions]

10WS1.2 Use precise language, action verbs, sensory details, appropriate modifiers, and the active rather than the passive voice. [3 questions]

10WS1.4 Develop the main ideas within the body of the composition through supporting evidence (e.g., scenarios, commonly held beliefs, hypotheses, definitions). [2 questions]

10WS1.5 Synthesize information from multiple sources and identify complexities and discrepancies in the information and the different perspectives found in each medium (e.g., almanacs, microfiche, news sources, in-depth field studies, speeches, journals, technical documents). [1 question]

10WS1.9 Revise writing to improve the logic and coherence of the organization and controlling perspective, the precision of word choice, and the tone by taking into consideration the audience, purpose, and formality of the context. [3 questions]

Read this passage from a previous CAHSEE administration and the discussion and questions that follow.

ROUGH DRAFT

Appreciating the Forgotten

(1) Can you name a famous inventor? (2) Many of the world's inventors have helped improve our day-to-day lives and are well remembered, Alexander Graham Bell for the telephone, Benjamin Franklin for bifocals, and Thomas Alva Edison for the lightbulb. (3) However, many other inventors' names have been forgotten despite their remarkable accomplishments.

(4) For example, who was Ezra J. Warner? (5) Back in 1858, he was the first person to patent a can opener. (6) Although it was effective, it was also dangerous to use and didn't make it into households until 1870, when William Lyman introduced a model that was just as effective but much safer.

(7) Susan Hibbard's invention didn't transform the world, but it did make a difference for other women inventors. (8) She took old turkey feathers and bound them together to make the first feather duster. (9) When she went to get the patent for it in 1876, however, she had to battle in court to prove it was her idea. (10) Eventually, Hibbard won the patent for her invention. (11) Her fight helped other women gain confidence in their ideas, and their right to patent them.

(12) Alice H. Parker patented a furnace that could heat individual rooms of a building at different temperatures. (13) Both energy and money were saved by Parker's furnace, since the invention allowed people to heat only the rooms needed at a given time.

(14) These inventors, their creations certainly improving the lives of many people, may not have received worldwide fame for their achievements.

59C-2

L259C002

Sample CAHSEE question
Which sentence would BEST begin Paragraph 1?

A   An invention is made when an inventor discovers how to solve a problem.

B   Many inventions have proven to be unnecessary and sometimes dangerous.

C   Inventors have created many amazing devices throughout history.

D   There have been a lot of inventions that have helped people.

Strategy
Be aware of the overall subject matter of a passage when selecting the *best* opening sentence. Avoid a self-evident definition which would not capture anyone's attention or make one want to continue reading. Avoid an off-topic option since the passage is about forgotten inventors, not inventions. Avoid a concluding statement. This should lead you directly to the correct answer.

L259C004

Sample CAHSEE question
Read the sentence from the passage.

> Both energy and money were saved by Parker's furnace, since the invention allowed people to heat only the rooms needed at a given time.

What is the BEST way to state the information in the underlined part of the sentence?

A   Parker's furnace saved both energy and money,

B   Saving both energy and money was Parker's furnace,

C   Saved by Parker's furnace were both energy and money,

D   Both energy and money have been saved by Parker's furnace,

Strategy
The question asks which is the *best* restatement of the underlined portion of the sentence. Notice that three options are written in the passive voice. The correct answer is the only option in the active voice. The active voice is considered the *best* choice. If you do not remember what active voice and passive voice are, you should review these distinctions. Compare these two sentences: **A** He threw the ball. **B** The ball was thrown by him. **A** is in the active voice because someone is performing an action. **B** is in the passive voice because an object is receiving an action.

L259C007

Sample CAHSEE question

Which is the BEST way to revise the sentence labeled 11?

A   Women were soon being granted more patents because of their confidence in their ideas.

B   Gaining confidence in their ideas and their right to patent were other women of the day.

C   Soon, women were gaining confidence in their ideas and confidence in their right to patent them.

D   Her fight helped other women gain confidence in their ideas and their right to patent them.

Strategy

In order to determine the *best* way to revise sentences, look at all four options and try to offer some evaluation of their strengths as well as weaknesses. Notice that option **A** is stated in the passive voice. Option **B** is a very awkward sentence with the subject tacked on to the end of the sentence. Option **C** is a very wordy sentence because six words are needlessly repeated within the sentence. There is only one option that restates the original sentence in the most direct manner.

Read this passage from a previous CAHSEE administration and the discussion and questions that follow.

ROUGH DRAFT

The Amazing Earthworm

(1) The earthworm is quite amazing. (2) When you spot earthworms lying on the sidewalk after a big rain, they probably all look similar to you. (3) But in fact, there are more than forty thousand kinds of worms and almost three thousand types of earthworms alone. (4) Australia has one called <u>Magoscolides Australis</u> that can grow to be 10 feet long!

(5) The structure of the earthworm is interesting. (6) The outside of its body is divided into approximately one hundred segments. (7) However, even with all those parts, the earthworm has no eyes. (8) Its body produces slime. (9) The inside of the earthworm is mostly stomach. (10) It has five pairs of hearts and a brain the size of a grain of sand.

(11) Earthworms do quite a bit for our environment. (12) When earthworms eat organic matter, they digest it in the stomach and excrete it as "castings." (13) Worm castings are a main component of dirt. (14) It's the earthworm that gives us our rich soil for plant growth.

97A

L197A005

Sample CAHSEE question
Which of the following sentences provides additional support for the main idea of Paragraph 3?

A Earthworms come to the surface when it rains.

B Earthworms decompose matter at a faster rate than landfills do.

C Earthworms create a series of tunnels through the dirt.

D Earthworms prefer to eat fruit and vegetable scraps.

Strategy
Notice that the question asks for additional support for a particular paragraph. Make sure you have correctly identified the overall subject matter of a paragraph in order to answer these types of questions. Although three options are all true statements about earthworms, only one option deals with the subject matter of Paragraph 3.

L197A007

Sample CAHSEE question
What would be the BEST source of information on Australian earthworms?

A a Web site for a company selling earthworms

B a magazine article entitled "Earthworms: the Farmer's Friend"

C a book entitled *Earthworms From Around the World*

D an Internet site on soil management using earthworms

Strategy
The question asks about the *best* source of information about Australian earthworms. Some options *might* contain information about Australian earthworms, but notice that these do not mention locations. The correct answer does suggest that many locations throughout the world will be considered. Since Australia is a continent with its own unique life forms, one option more than the others would most likely contain information about Australian earthworms.

For more practice on these types of questions, go to the Released Test Questions at http://www.cde.ca.gov/ta/tg/hs/resources.asp.

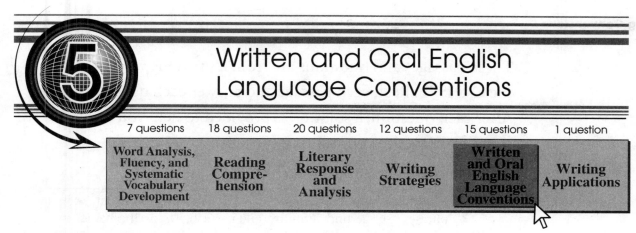

Written and Oral English Language Conventions

7 questions	18 questions	20 questions	12 questions	15 questions	1 question
Word Analysis, Fluency, and Systematic Vocabulary Development	Reading Comprehension	Literary Response and Analysis	Writing Strategies	Written and Oral English Language Conventions	Writing Applications

These are the 3 CAHSEE Writing Conventions Standards.

The CAHSEE uses 15 multiple-choice questions to test your knowledge of the writing conventions standards. In this section, you do not write any essays, but you answer questions about writing. You will be expected to recognize proper sentence construction, paragraph structure, grammar, usage, and punctuation.

Grammar can be tricky. You have to learn many, many rules — remember them. California's content standards expect you to know how to follow the conventions (that means rules) for punctuation, capitalization, grammar, and usage. So let's see what we can do to help you through this part of the test. Some of the questions focus on choosing (and using) the right verb tenses. Others refer to misplaced modifiers.

You may be wondering, "What's a subordinate clause?" "Do modifiers have a proper place?" "How do I control grammar?" "I never heard of parallel structure." Quit worrying. Maybe you didn't quite understand phrases and clauses, and maybe you don't remember modifiers, but with a little common sense and a few rules, you can get through this. Trust us!

These passages and questions are from a previous version of the CAHSEE. Read each passage and answer each question. After each question, a solution is provided to help you understand and practice your writing conventions skills.

10WC1.1 Identify and correctly use clauses (e.g., main and subordinate), phrases (e.g., gerund, infinitive, and participial), and mechanics of punctuation (e.g., semicolons, colons, ellipses, hyphens). [5 questions]

10WC1.2 Understand sentence construction (e.g., parallel structure, subordination, proper placement of modifiers) and proper English usage (e.g., consistency of verb tenses). [5 questions]

10WC1.3 Demonstrate an understanding of proper English usage and control of grammar, paragraph and sentence structure, diction, and syntax. [5 questions]

L10SA069

Sample CAHSEE question
That collection of essays John wants on the bottom shelf.

A   John wants them, that collection of essays

B   John wants that collection of essays

C   Wanted by John, that collection of essays

D   Leave as is.

Strategy
You must carefully analyze all the options in order to do well with these questions. Notice that one option is a very awkward sentence with a double object, "them" as well as "that collection of essays." Another reason to eliminate this option is because "them" is plural while "that collection of essays" is singular. Another option should be eliminated because it is not a complete sentence. The last option asks you to accept the original sentence as is, but the original sentence is a very awkward sentence because it does not have a normal word order. The object comes before the subject which is followed by the verb. The correct answer is a smooth sentence using a normal subject, verb, object word order.

L10SA065

Sample CAHSEE question
<u>Walking and to jog and to cycle</u> **are activities many people can enjoy.**

A   To walk, and jogging and cycle

B   To walk, to jog, and cycling

C   Walking, jogging, and cycling

D   Leave as is.

Strategy
This question tests your knowledge of parallel structure. But in order to answer these types of questions, it is important to know the many forms verbs can take. A verb stated as "to do something," like "to jog" or "to walk" is the infinitive. A verb ending in -ing but treated as a noun, like "jogging is fun," is the gerund. Notice in this question that the sentence has a gerund and two infinitives as its subject. Parallel structure happens when important ideas within a sentence are stated in the same form. The correct answer presents all three activities that form the subject of the sentence as gerunds.

L00SA100

Sample CAHSEE question
While Sara visited <u>with Sam: she finished</u> her science project.

A   with Sam. She finished

B   with Sam; she finished

C   with Sam, she finished

D   Leave as is.

Strategy
This question tests your ability to distinguish dependent and independent clauses within a sentence and how to correctly punctuate the sentence. It is important to understand what dependent and independent clauses are. An independent clause can be removed from the rest of a sentence, and it will still be a complete sentence. A dependent clause *depends* on the rest of the sentence in order to express a complete idea. "While Sara visited with Sam: she finished her science project." In this sentence, "she finished her science project" is a complete sentence. "While Sara visited with Sam" does not express a complete thought. A dependent and independent clause must be joined with a comma in a sentence.

L10SA160

Sample CAHSEE question
My <u>sister a high school freshman,</u> is trying out for the school play.

A   sister, a high school freshman,

B   sister: a high school freshman

C   sister a high school freshman

D   Leave as is.

Strategy
This question requires you to know how to punctuate an appositive in a sentence. An appositive is a group of words that further describes a subject. Appositives are set off with commas. If it helps, remove everything between the commas: "My sister is trying out for the school play." The added information about "my sister," that she is "a high school freshman," is an appositive.

L10SA060

Sample CAHSEE question
Mr. Forbes needs the following items for his <u>cooking class flour, salt, and a variety of spices</u>.

A   cooking class: flour, salt, and a variety of spices

B   cooking class; flour, salt, and a variety of spices

C   cooking class, flour, salt, and a variety of spices

D   Leave as is.

Strategy
Remember that a list is often set off with a colon. The semicolon can join independent clauses. A comma is too weak to set off a list. Look carefully at the original sentence before selecting the correct answer.

L10SA077

Sample CAHSEE question
We're <u>sorry to bother you, but we need</u> to ask you a question.

A   sorry, to bother you but we need

B   sorry to bother you, but, we need

C   sorry to bother you but we need

D   Leave as is.

Strategy
Remember that a comma and a conjunction join two independent clauses. Carefully study the original sentence and the options.

L10SA134

Sample CAHSEE question

Akia told us about her safari across the plains of East Africa in our geography class.

A   In our geography class, Akia told us about her safari across the plains of East Africa.

B   Akia told us about her safari in our geography class across the plains of East Africa.

C   In our geography class Akia told about her safari across the plains of East Africa to us.

D   Leave as is.

Strategy

Misplaced modifiers can be a lot of fun. The original sentence implies that the safari is happening in geography class. One option implies that the geography class is across the plains of East Africa. In another option, "to us" is dangling at the end of that sentence, just begging to be moved. Clearly only one option makes everything sound right.

L00SA136

Sample CAHSEE question

The green backpack has _____ pockets than the blue one.

A   least

B   less

C   fewest

D   fewer

Strategy

Is it "less" or "fewer"? There is a difference. If it can be counted, it's fewer. For example, I have fewer books now because I have less interest in reading. I can assign a number to the books I have, but I can't assign a number to the interest I have. Also you need to know that adjectives can express degrees of comparison. The word "than" in the original sentence lets you know a degree of comparison is needed. Since two objects are being compared, you also should know which form of an adjective to use. Now you can find the correct answer.

L00SA091

Sample CAHSEE question
Tam left the decision up to _____.

A we

B us

C she

D they

Strategy

Some pronouns are used as subjects while other pronouns are used as objects. The correct answer uses a pronoun as the object of the preposition "to." If you're not sure, try it out. Is it "Give it to *we*" or "Give it to *she*" or "Give it to *they*"? In these examples, the pronouns sound wrong because the pronouns are supposed to be subjects. Now try this: "*We* give it to you." In English grammar this is known as pronoun case.

L10SA073

Sample CAHSEE question
_____ going to sample different kinds of juice, aren't they?

A Their

B There

C They're

D They

Strategy

Be sure to distinguish meaning. Homophones are words that sound alike but have different meanings. The correct answer is a contraction of "they are."

L20SA101

Sample CAHSEE question
Uncle Yary often <u>said; "My way is the best way."</u>

A said "My way is the best way."

B said, "My way is the best way".

C said, "My way is the best way."

D Leave as is.

Strategy

This question tests your knowledge of how to properly punctuate a direct quotation within a sentence. Remember that a direct quotation is set off by a comma before the beginning of the direct quotation, and the final punctuation mark goes inside the closed quotation marks.

For more practice on these types of questions, go to the Released Test Questions at http://www.cde.ca.gov/ta/tg/hs/resources.asp.

Writing Applications

7 questions   18 questions   20 questions   12 questions   15 questions   1 question

| Word Analysis, Fluency, and Systematic Vocabulary Development | Reading Compre-hension | Literary Response and Analysis | Writing Strategies | Written and Oral English Language Conventions | Writing Applications |

On the CAHSEE, you will be expected to write one essay. The writing task for the essay will require you to do any one of the following types of writing:

- ◆ Biographical narrative
- ◆ Response to literature
- ◆ Expository essay
- ◆ Persuasive essay
- ◆ Business letter

The CAHSEE will test your knowledge of 5 Writing Applications Standards. They are:

> **10WA2.1** Write biographical narratives:
> a. Relate a sequence of events and communicate the signifi-cance of the events to the audience.
> b. Locate scenes and incidents in specific places.
> c. Describe with concrete sensory details the sights, sounds, and smells of a scene and the specific actions, movements, ges-tures, and feelings of the characters; use interior monologue to depict the characters' feelings.
> d. Pace the presentation of actions to accommodate changes in time and mood.
> e. Make effective use of descriptions of appearance, images, shifting perspectives, and sensory details.

> **10WA2.2** Write responses to literature:
> a. Demonstrate a comprehensive grasp of the significant ideas of literary works.
> b. Support important ideas and viewpoints through accurate and detailed references to the text or to other works.
> c. Demonstrate awareness of the author's use of stylistic devices and an appreciation of the effects created.
> d. Identify and assess the impact of perceived ambiguities, nu-ances, and complexities within the text.

Writing Applications

10WA2.3 Write expository compositions, including analytical essays and research reports:
a. Marshal evidence in support of a thesis and related claims, including information on all relevant perspectives.
b. Convey information and ideas from primary and secondary sources accurately and coherently.
c. Make distinctions between the relative value and significance of specific data, facts, and ideas.
d. ~~Include visual aids by employing appropriate technology to organize and record information on charts, maps, and graphs.~~
e. Anticipate and address readers' potential misunderstandings, biases, and expectations.
f. Use technical terms and notations accurately.

10WA2.4 Write persuasive compositions:
a. Structure ideas and arguments in a sustained and logical fashion.
b. Use specific rhetorical devices to support assertions (e.g., appeal to logic through reasoning; appeal to emotion or ethical belief; relate a personal anecdote, case study, or analogy).
c. Clarify and defend positions with precise and relevant evidence, including facts, expert opinions, quotations, and expressions of commonly accepted beliefs and logical reasoning.
d. Address readers' concerns, counterclaims, biases, and expectations.

10WA2.5 Write business letters:
a. Provide clear and purposeful information and address the intended audience appropriately.
b. Use appropriate vocabulary, tone, and style to take into account the nature of the relationship with, and the knowledge and interests of, the recipients.
c. Highlight central ideas or images.
d. Follow a conventional style with page formats, fonts, and spacing that contribute to the documents' readability and impact.

In this section, different types of writing are discussed and illustrated. They include writing tasks and sample student responses from previous CAHSEEs. You should practice these writing types often. You probably are writing in school, but another useful activity is to keep a journal and write about people you know (biographical narrative), things you have learned (expository essay), or opinions you have on any subject (persuasive essay).

BIOGRAPHICAL ESSAYS

When you write a biographical narrative, you are writing about a real person who is important to you. You will want the reader to know why this person is important to you and why you feel about this person the way you do. One way to do this is to tell stories or anecdotes about this person.

You could start by making a chart. The chart might have two columns—one for a list of adjectives that describe the person, for example, with a list of traits that you admire and the other for a list of stories (anecdotes or examples) that demonstrate or explain how or why you feel that way. The chart below shows some notes the author made before writing about her dad. In the first column, she put the words *intelligent, loving,* and *funny.* In the second column she wrote a few notes about some stories that she thinks will show different ways in which her dad was intelligent, loving, and funny. When she is ready to write, she can focus on just one of these, or two, or all three. If the time to write is limited, she might just choose to tell the stories about how intelligent he is and how much she respects, admires, and even envies his intelligence.

My Dad

Trait	Story
Intelligent	Story about when he was in elem. School. Able to read and remember, photo mind Knowledgeable about everything
Loving	Would do anything for me and mom Left little notes in crazy places for mom when he went on trips
Funny and fun-loving	Great story teller Told shaggy dog stories Liked to play games (not sports) The ultimate Dodger fan

In your essay, you will want to include something from each item on the following list, which is from the California content standards:

- Explain why this person is important to you and give examples.
- Be specific. Don't just say the person is interesting. Let your reader *see the person.* Show the person doing something interesting.
- Include sensory details: sights, sounds, and smells.
- Decide how much time to spend on each part of your story so that you are able to include everything you want to say.
- Make sure the reader can see this person. What does she look like? What does he do?

Now you pick someone, make a chart, and write your biographical narrative. When you finish, ask a teacher or someone else to read it and comment on it for you.

RESPONSES TO LITERATURE

Before you can "respond to literature," you have to read something. The California content standards for writing responses to literature require that you are able to:

- ***Demonstrate a comprehensive grasp of the significant ideas of literary works.*** What are the main ideas? What is the author saying? Why (or why not) is what the author is saying important?
- ***Support important ideas and viewpoints through accurate and detailed references to the text or to other works.*** How do you know what the author's ideas are? Can you quote from the text to prove what you say?
- ***Demonstrate awareness of the author's use of stylistic devices and an appreciation of the effects created.*** Does the author use figurative language? Give an example. Does the author use symbolism? How is the symbolism used? Does the author use words that help you to see, smell, taste, hear, or feel the setting or scene? Does the author use words that make you angry or sad or excited or scared?
- ***Identify and assess the impact of perceived ambiguities, nuances, and complexities within the text.*** This one sounds complicated, doesn't it? But don't worry. The best writers usually say something that makes you think, makes you question, makes you wonder. Just go with it. Ask the questions. Try to figure it out. Don't look for a *right* answer—there may not be a right answer. It's all right to talk about and write about the things that confuse you.

> In the pages that follow, you will read a passage (literature), and write an essay (response) based on that passage.

Let's examine a prompt that appeared on the CAHSEE during a previous administration. First you will need to read the story "The Hiking Trip."

The Hiking Trip

"I never wanted to come on this stupid old hiking trip anyway!" His voice echoed, shrill and panicked, across the narrow canyon. His father stopped, chest heaving with the effort of the climb, and turned to look at the boy.

"This is hard on you, son, I know. But you've got to come through with courage and a level head."

"But I'm scared! I don't even want to have courage!" he retorted. He jerked his head the other way and wiped his eyes across his arm.

"If not courage, fine," his father replied sternly. "Then have enough love for your brother to think this through!" He pulled a bandana from his back pocket and tied it around his neck. Then he gently placed his hand on the boy's shoulder and continued, more softly this time. "Now, I don't know if I can make it without stopping every so often. And we just don't have the time to stop. You're young, but you're strong and fast. Do you remember the way back from here to the road, if you had to go alone?"

Jeff flashed back to the agonizing scene of his seventeen-year-old brother at their campsite that morning. He'd been bitten by a snake

yesterday during a rough hike through very rocky terrain. By the time they returned to their tents, he was limping badly. Then this morning he couldn't put on his boots, and the pain seemed to be getting worse. He needed medical attention right away, so leaving him there was their only choice.

"Jeffrey? Jeffrey, could you do it? Could you make it to the road without me if you had to?"

Jeff blinked and looked past his father's eyes to the end of the canyon, several miles away. He nodded slowly as the path and the plan began to take hold in his mind. "What was the name of that little town we stopped in to get matches, Dad?"

His father smiled and replied, "Flint. After we left Flint, we parked at the side of the road a few miles out of town. When you see which way our car is facing, you'll know that the town is back the other direction." Jeff thought about this and then nodded. They both drank water and then continued scrambling over the rocks.

Nothing was as pretty as it had seemed when they first hiked this way to their campsite. Before, the boulders and rocks had been an interesting challenge. Now, they were obstacles that threatened their footing and their velocity. Overhanging limbs had earlier been natural curiosities in the cliffs. But now they were nature's weapons, slapping and scratching the boy and the man who crashed by and pushed through as quickly as they could.

Stone by stone, they made their way up the canyon. Jeff's father grew smaller and smaller in the distance. "He must be stopping a lot," Jeff thought. He waved to him from a bend in the canyon wall. His father waved back. Jeff turned and made the final ascent up an easier slope toward the road and spotted his father's car. He lurched toward it, half stumbling, and leaned on the hood, breathless.

"Can't stop," he thought. "Mark's in big trouble. Gotta keep going." The fast, loud thudding in his ears was deafening, and as he pulled himself upright, he was surprised as a car sped by, heading toward Flint. "Hey, mister!" he shouted, waving both arms. He began to walk, faster and faster until he was jogging. Then he quickly crossed the highway and broke into a full-speed run, holding his left arm straight out, his thumb up.

His chest was burning with every breath when he suddenly heard several loud honks from behind. He turned as the brakes squealed and saw "Bob's Towing & Repair, Flint" right behind him. "Jump in, boy! What's up?" Jeff explained between gasps as the truck picked up speed. The driver reached for his two-way radio as soon as he heard about Mark. "Better get the helicopter in there," he seemed to be shouting into his

hand. But Jeff wasn't sure about that because everything got fuzzy and then went black and quiet.

Hours later, Jeff opened his eyes to find strange surroundings and his father on a chair nearby.

"You're a hero, son," his father said with a smile. "You saved Mark."

"What happened?" Jeff asked through a wide yawn. "Where are we?"

"This is a motel room in Flint. You made it into town and sent the helicopter into the canyon after Mark. I can't tell you how happy I was when I saw it overhead. I'm so proud of you!"

Jeff sat up suddenly. "Where's Mark? Is he OK?"

"They airlifted him out and got him to the hospital. His leg's still in bad shape, but he's going to be just fine in a couple of days. Thanks to you, son."

Jeff's worried face relaxed as his father spoke. "How about you, Dad? How did you get out?"

"Well, I finally hiked myself out of that canyon and to the road. I won't be going back there any time soon. That's for sure. Anyway, I couldn't see the car, and as I headed for Flint I got lucky and was able to hitch a ride from a fellow named Bob in a tow truck."

Jeff laughed out loud. "I guess Bob makes a good living going up and down that road. I hope you gave him a good tip, Dad!"

157

Sample CAHSEE question
Writing Task

In the story "The Hiking Trip," the reader learns about the main character, Jeff. Jeff's personality and emotions are revealed through the actions and dialogue presented in the story.

Write an essay in which you describe the personality and emotions of Jeff, the main character. How do his personal characteristics add to the events in the story? How does the author reveal this information about Jeff in the story? Use details and examples from the story to support your ideas.

Checklist for Your Writing

The following checklist will help you do your best work. Make sure you:
- ❏ Carefully read the passage and the description of the task.
- ❏ Organize your writing with a strong introduction, body, and conclusion.
- ❏ Use specific details and examples from the passage to demonstrate your understanding of the main ideas and the author's purpose.
- ❏ Use precise language that is appropriate for your audience and purpose.
- ❏ Vary your sentences to make your writing interesting to read.
- ❏ Check for mistakes in grammar, spelling, punctuation, capitalization, and sentence formation.

(10WA2.2)

Make sure you know exactly what the prompt asks you to do. Does it ask you to summarize the story? No, it doesn't. The prompt asks you to write about Jeff's personality and emotions. How would you describe his personality? What were his emotions? What in the story tells you this? If you make a simple grid, you can organize your thoughts before you begin to write.

Jeff's personality/emotions	Evidence from the story
Courageous	At the beginning, he didn't think he was courageous. Didn't want to be. Went on alone. "You're a hero, son."
Loving	Did it for his brother "Mark's in big trouble. Gotta keep going."
Determined	Kept going "His chest was burning."

With this simple grid, you can focus on what you write about Jeff, not on retelling the story.

Now look at a sample student essay, one that earned a score of 3 (out of 4) on the CAHSEE.

Student Essay

To understand who Jeff is, you have to realize what he has to go through in the story. In the beginning, Jeff is afraid to hike and doesn't want to have the courage to climb the mountain. After Jeff's dad says, "If not courage, fine. Then have enough love for your brother," Jeff realizes that he has to do it to save his brother's life. He becomes determined to find help. He thinks about how badly his brother needs medical attention.

Jeff becomes so determined to get help, he begins to climb faster and faster until he passes up his dad. He says to himself "Can't stop, Mark's in big trouble." This shows how his love for his brother has substituted for the courage that he did want to have. Do you think that his love for his brother gives him the courage or the will to climb the mountain and get help for Mark.

Hours later after Mark is rescued, Jeff wakes up but doesn't know what had happened. His father tells him that he's a hero and that he saved his brothers life. He had pushed himself to the limits trying to get help for Mark. His love for Mark had given him the will, the determination, and the courage to get over his fear and climb the mountain for help.

Commentary

The writer addressed all parts of the writing task. He described Jeff's personality and emotions, quoted from the text, and showed how his personality and emotions added to the events of the story. (He did forget to mention the name of the story. When you write your response to literature, don't forget to include the title of the piece!)

What could the writer have done to make this essay even better? This paper did not receive a 4 because of its chronological arrangement; the paper summarizes the story instead of focusing on the main character, Jeff. Although the second and third paragraphs implicitly, indirectly, give evidence of Jeff's character, the scorers felt that this should be more explicit, more direct.

The writer also forgot his audience. In the first sentence, he directs his words to "you." He does it again in the second paragraph. "Do you think that his love for his brother gives him the courage or the will to climb the mountain and get help for Mark?" I am writing this study guide to you, so I refer to you in practically every paragraph because I want you to pass the CAHSEE. Who is the audience for this piece on "The Hiking Trip"?

One more tip. Strong beginnings can signify strong papers. Try starting with dialogue or a description, something that grabs the reader right away. Do we really care "who Jeff is" with this beginning? These sentences, quoted from the story, might make a good beginning. "Jeffrey, could you do it? Could you make it to the road without me if you had to?"

EXPOSITION

<u>Expository essays</u>: Exposition is a type of writing that explains, gives information, or clarifies an idea. This is the most common type of writing in school and in life. When your teachers ask you to write a report or a research paper or a summary, they are asking you to write exposition. Exposition is also used as a part of other types of writing. For example, in writing a story, you may be writing exposition to set up the plot, the characters, and their conflicts. Exposition is most often nonfiction, meaning that it deals with real people, things, events, and places. According to the California content standards for expository writing, you should know how to do these things:

- Gather evidence in support of your subject.
- Use primary (first-hand) sources and secondary sources (newspapers) accurately.
- Distinguish between information and the significance of the data.
- Know how to use and include visual aids—charts, maps, graphs, technology.
- Be aware of your audience, anticipating misunderstandings.
- Use subject-specific terms accurately.

Let's examine a prompt that appeared on the CAHSEE.

L0000064

<u>**Writing Task**</u>

By the time students enter high school, they have learned about many moments in history that have influenced our world today. Think about a moment in history you studied and consider its importance.

Write a composition in which you discuss a moment in history. Share its importance in today's world. Be sure to support the moment with details and examples.

Checklist for Your Writing

The following checklist will help you do your best work. Make sure you:
- ❑ Read the description of the task carefully.
- ❑ Use specific details and examples to fully support your ideas.
- ❑ Organize your writing with a strong introduction, body, and conclusion.
- ❑ Choose specific words that are appropriate for your audience and purpose.
- ❑ Vary your sentences to make your writing interesting to read.
- ❑ Check for mistakes in grammar, spelling, punctuation, and sentence formation.

(10WA2.3)

What do the writers of the prompt ask you to do first? They ask you to think about a time in history that you have studied, to think about why that time in history was important. Then they ask you to write about that time in history, telling why it is important in today's world, and to support what you say with details and examples.
So how many things do you have to do?

An organizational chart can organize your thoughts.

❑ **Divide your paper into three columns.**

❑ **In the first column, describe the event or events. (You may want to list two or three to see which one you know the most about. You should pick a topic that you know something about so that you have something to say. It could be something you have just studied in school or something that has just happened in current events.)**

❑ **In the second column, write some notes about what the world was like before the event.**

❑ **In the third column, write about how this event has changed the world or why it is still important in today's world. In this column you need to list many examples to prove the event's importance. If you can't think of enough examples, you should choose another event.**

❑ **When your chart is complete, you are ready to write.**

Again, a reminder that the writing itself is what's important here. You are not being asked to show what you know about history. If you are hazy about details, admit that in the writing.

Event/description	World before/at time of event	Why important in today's world
Man on moon	Unsuccessful attempts	Americans can do anything they want Americans are great Gave Americans courage Gave Americans respect
Invention of auto	Horse-drawn carriages Rode horseback Walked Took forever to travel People did not travel Uncomfortable Trains didn't go everywhere	People can live farther from their workplace Created an urban/sub-urban society Highways, maps, freeways, toll roads, high speeds Comfortable Independence

Following is a released student essay, one that earned a score of 3 (out of 4) on the CAHSEE. The writer chose "man setting foot on the moon" as the event. He does not know much about this event.

Student Essay

One of the most important days in history so far is the day that man set foot on the moon. This was not only important in U.S. history, but it was important to everywhere else in the world too. This amazing achievement showed Americans that they can do anything they want, if they try hard enough, and it showed other countries how great we really are.

The day that man set foot on the moon was a very exciting day. A lot of people didn't believe that it really happened because it was so amazing. But when everyone realized that it had really happened, it gave them the courage to strive for their goals and achieve them.

For years before man stepped on the moon, other countries had been trying to and were unsuccessful. But, America was able to. This made the other countries have so much more respect for us.

When man set foot on the moon, it was honestly one of the most important days in history because of what took place as a result of it.

Commentary

Notice that this writer has written an introduction that makes it clear he is going to write about the moment in history when "man set foot on the moon." His reason is that this "amazing achievement showed Americans they can do anything they want." It also showed other countries what a great country the U.S. is. Consider what this writer might have done to make his introduction more interesting. Perhaps he could have started with a description of that moment when Neil Armstrong "set foot on the moon" and the words he said that have gone down in history.

In the second paragraph he says the day was "exciting" and "amazing." He says that this moment "gave them [Americans] courage to strive for their goals and achieve them."

The writer tells us in the third paragraph that because of this moment, other countries gained respect for America. He concludes, "... it was... one of the most important days in history."

If you want to practice, write an expository essay to this prompt. Choose a period of history you know well, and recall all the things you have learned about writing expository essays. Ask a teacher to read it and comment on it for you. Expository essays will be scored using the same rubric as biographical narratives. If you would like to read a sample student essay for each other score point you can go to http://www.cde.ca.gov/ta/tg/hs/.

PERSUASIVE ESSAYS

When you turn the page in your test booklet to the writing prompt, it won't be labeled as a persuasive essay, but you will know if you are being asked to write a persuasive essay by reading the description of the task carefully. Persuasive essays ask you to defend a position or issue you support. An issue is something about which people disagree.

As you prepare to write, you will need to take a stand on the issue the prompt provides. Do you agree or disagree? Decide and then make two columns. In one column, list all the reasons why you support your position, why you believe as you do. Try to come up with at least three reasons. In the other column list all the reasons why an opponent might disagree with you. These are counter-arguments. Try again for at least three. Consider this kind of writing as a debate on paper.

You are almost ready to write. When you write your arguments, you want the two most powerful points to be first and last.

Place a star by those arguments. Now you are ready to write. In order to meet the California content standards, your persuasive essay will need to do the following:

- Have a logical structure. Put your most powerful arguments first and last.
- Appeal to the reader's logic or emotions.
- Tell a personal story or someone else's story or make a comparison. This may be a good way to start.
- Use fact, expert opinions, or both to clarify your position. You want to demonstrate that this is not merely your opinion but an opinion that other thoughtful individuals share.
- Address the reader's concerns and arguments. Use your list of counter-arguments to help you do this.

In an effective persuasive essay, the writer's opinion is clear. Check that your opinion and reasoning are clear and understandable. You might also want to consider using a hook to involve readers immediately—a meaningful quote, an interesting anecdote, a puzzling question, or a dramatic statistic—or several of these combined. Finally, don't forget to include the arguments of those who disagree with you—then, explain why your arguments are stronger.

Let's examine a prompt that previously appeared on the CAHSEE.

L000060

Sample CAHSEE question
Some students at your school expressed an interest in making the school more attractive by getting rid of the trash on the school grounds.

Write a persuasive essay for your school paper in which you convince the readers of the importance of getting rid of the trash and making the school more attractive. Convince your readers through the use of specific reasons and examples.

Checklist for Your Writing

The following checklist will help you do your best work. Make sure you:
- ❏ Read the description of the task carefully.
- ❏ Organize your writing with a strong introduction, body, and conclusion.
- ❏ State your position, support it with specific examples, and address the reader's concerns.
- ❏ Use words that are appropriate for your audience and purpose.
- ❏ Vary your sentences to make your writing interesting to read.
- ❏ Check for mistakes in grammar, spelling, punctuation, capitalization, and sentence formation.

(10WA2.4)

Following is a sample student essay, one that earned a score of 3 (out of 4) on the CAHSEE.

Student Essay

Nobody would like it if people stopped picking up trash and let our school become filled with trash. It is very important to keep our school clean to provide an appropriate learning environment. If everyone would help out our school would look more attractive.

A clean school campus would offer a nicer and appropriate learning environment. A dirty school makes it harder to concentrate on school work. If trash covered the campus students might be looking out classroom windows for what awaits them after class and wondering why someone is not cleaning it up. A clean school would help the students concentrate so grades might raise not only making the school look better on the outside but academically as well.

No one enjoys being in a dirty environment. Before school, snack, lunch, and after school would be much less enjoy-able to both the students and faculty if our campus was dirty. People do not like eating in trash filled lunch areas and so there would be more students leaving school permitted or not for lunch. Basically, students and teachers would not be able to stand being in a dirty environment during school hours.

In conclusion living environments are kept clean and so it is equally important to keep learning environments clean as well. Both the students and faculty spend large portions of their days here so to make school a little better and more attractive our school needs to be kept clean. It would be easy if everyone just did their part.

Commentary

When you read the first paragraph of this essay, you know immediately that the writer wants everyone to help keep the school environment attractive, and in the following paragraphs, the writer gives reasons why: to present an appropriate learning environment; to make the school a more enjoyable place. The writer ends with "It would be easy if everyone just did their part."

The writer has met the basic demands of persuasive writing. The writer has an introduction, body, and conclusion; the writer has stated a clear position; the writer has used a variety of sentence structures; the writer has addressed the reader's concerns.

What could the writer have done to make this piece more interesting to the reader? What would you advise? How about beginning with a great description of a dirty campus (or a clean one)? How about some anecdotes, little stories that describe what students who care can do? What about some dialogue between two students about the state of the campus? When a writer adds these kinds of dramatic examples, the writing becomes more powerful.

Why don't you try writing your own essay on this topic for practice? Read the prompt again, and write a persuasive essay in which you convince your readers of the importance of getting rid of the trash on your school grounds and making your school more attractive. Persuasive essays will be scored using the rubric for these essays which you will find on page 117.

BUSINESS LETTERS

When writing business letters, your purpose may be to inform, to suggest, to complain, to argue, to persuade, or to commend. Sometimes a business letter is an expository piece of writing about buying a product that didn't work: You explain how the product was defective and demand your money back. A business letter might also be a persuasive piece of writing: Students deserve clean school restrooms, but your school's restrooms are a mess. You write a letter to the Board of Education to persuade the Board to take action on this problem. A business letter might be a biographical piece of writing: If you are asked to write a letter of recommendation, you will have to describe the person you are recommending and tell how he or she would be perfect for the job.

According to the California content standards, you should be able to:

- Read the prompt carefully. What does the prompt ask you to do? Begin with a salutation, "Dear _____" or "To Whom It May Concern:" Sign your name at the end of your business letter.
- Remember your audience, the person who will be receiving the letter, and use language that the person will appreciate and pay attention to. Don't use slang when addressing the Board of Education, for example. On the other hand, you might use some slang if you're requesting a free CD from your favorite musician's record company.
- Keep the letter short and to the point. Make your central ideas clear.
- Remember that if you want to make a good impression, you will need to pay attention to format and spacing as well as spelling, grammar, and punctuation.

Look at the practice persuasive essay you wrote about picking up trash on the school grounds. Can you turn that essay into a letter? Of course you can. Who would be your audience? The students at your high school—the same audience you had when you wrote for the school newspaper. It shouldn't take much effort to take those ideas and put them in the form of a business letter. Try it.

[Note: No sample student essays have been released for business letters.]

So there you have it. You have finished this study guide that was written just for you. We hope it will help you pass the California High School Exit Exam. If you still have questions, your teachers can help you. Perhaps your parents or guardians can help as well. Everyone wants you to succeed. Just remember to read carefully, reread when you have questions, and use logic and common sense. Don't forget to use the "practice test" in this Study Guide as you prepare for the real thing.

Every chance you get, read and write for your own enjoyment. Talk to others about the books you read. Keep a journal. This isn't only about succeeding on a test or in your English class. This is about enriching your life!

California High School Exit Examination

SCORING GUIDE

Response to Literary/Expository Text

4 **The response—**
- demonstrates a *thoughtful,* comprehensive grasp of the text.
- accurately and coherently provides *specific* textual details and examples to support the thesis and main ideas.
- demonstrates a *clear* understanding of the ambiguities, nuances, and complexities of the text.
- provides a *variety* of sentence types and uses *precise, descriptive* language.
- contains *few, if any, errors* in the conventions* of the English language. (Errors are generally first-draft in nature.)

Response to informational passages:
- *thoughtfully* anticipates and addresses the reader's potential misunderstandings, biases, and expectations.

Response to literary passages:
- clearly demonstrates an awareness of the author's use of literary and/or stylistic devices.

3 **The response—**
- demonstrates a comprehensive grasp of the text.
- accurately and coherently provides *general* textual details and examples to support the thesis and main ideas.
- demonstrates a *general* understanding of the ambiguities, nuances, and complexities of the text.
- provides a *variety* of sentence types and uses *some descriptive* language.
- may contain *some errors* in the conventions* of the English language. (Errors do **not** interfere with the reader's understanding of the essay.)

Response to informational passages:
- anticipates and addresses the reader's potential misunderstandings, biases, and expectations.

Response to literary passages:
- demonstrates an awareness of the author's use of literary and/or stylistic devices.

2 **The response—**
- demonstrates a *limited* grasp of the text.
- provides few, *if any,* textual details and examples to support the thesis and main ideas.
- demonstrates *limited, or no* understanding of the ambiguities, nuances, and complexities of the text.
- provides *few, if any,* types of sentences and uses *basic, predictable* language.
- may contain *several* errors in the conventions* of the English language. (Errors may interfere with the reader's understanding of the essay.)

Response to informational passages:
- *may* address the reader's potential misunderstandings, biases, and expectations, but in a limited manner.

Response to literary passages:
- *may* demonstrate an awareness of the author's use of literary and/or stylistic devices.

1 The response—

- demonstrates *minimal* grasp of the text.
- may provide **no** textual details and examples to support the thesis and main ideas.
- may demonstrate **no** understanding of the ambiguities, nuances, and complexities of the text.
- may provide **no** sentence variety and uses *limited* vocabulary.
- may contain *serious errors* in the conventions* of the English language. (Errors interfere with the reader's understanding of the essay.)

Response to informational passages:
- does **not** address the reader's potential misunderstandings, biases, and expectations.

Response to literary passages:
- does **not** demonstrate awareness of the author's use of literary and/or stylistic devices.

non-scorable: The code "NS" will appear on the student answer document for responses that are written in a language other than English, off-topic, illegible, unintelligible, or otherwise non-responsive to the writing task.

* *Conventions of the English language refer to grammar, punctuation, spelling, capitalization, and usage.*

This guide describes the attributes of student writing at each score point. Each paper receives the score that best fits the overall evidence provided by the student in response to the prompt. However, papers that do not meet the standard for conventions at a 4 or a 3 score point receive a score that is at most one point lower.

California High School Exit Examination

SCORING GUIDE

Response to Writing Prompt

4 The essay—
- provides a *meaningful* thesis that is responsive to the writing task.
- *thoroughly* supports the thesis and main ideas with *specific* details and examples.
- demonstrates a consistent tone and focus, and illustrates a *purposeful* control of organization.
- demonstrates a *clear* sense of audience.
- provides a *variety* of sentence types and uses *precise, descriptive* language.
- contains *few, if any, errors* in the conventions* of the English language. (Errors are generally first-draft in nature.)

A Persuasive Composition:
- states and maintains a position, *authoritatively* defends that position with precise and relevant evidence, and *convincingly* addresses the reader's concerns, biases, and expectations.

3 The essay—
- provides a thesis that is responsive to the writing task.
- supports the thesis and main ideas with details and examples.
- demonstrates a consistent tone and focus; and illustrates a control of organization.
- demonstrates a *general* sense of audience.
- provides a *variety* of sentence types and uses *some descriptive language.*
- may contain some errors in the conventions* of the English language. (Errors do **not** interfere with the reader's understanding of the essay.)

A Persuasive Composition:
- states and maintains a position, *generally* defends that position with precise and relevant evidence, and addresses the reader's concerns, biases, and expectations.

2 The essay—
- provides a thesis or main idea that is related to the writing task.
- supports the thesis or main idea(s) with *limited* details and/or examples.
- demonstrates an *inconsistent* tone and focus; and illustrates *little, if any,* control of organization.
- demonstrates *little* or **no** sense of audience.
- provides *few, if any,* types of sentence types, and *basic, predictable* language.
- may contain *several* errors in the conventions* of the English language. (Errors *may* interfere with the reader's understanding of the essay.)

A Persuasive Composition:
- defends a position with *little* evidence and *may* address the reader's concerns, biases, and expectations.

1 The essay—

- *may* provide a *weak* thesis or main idea that is related to the writing task.
- *fails* to support the thesis or main ideas with details and/or examples.
- demonstrates a *lack of* tone and focus; and illustrates *no* control of organization.
- may demonstrate *no* sense of audience.
- may provide *no* sentence variety and uses *limited* vocabulary.
- may contain *serious errors* in the conventions* of the English language. (Errors interfere with the reader's understanding of the essay.)

A Persuasive Composition:

- *fails* to defend a position with any evidence and *fails* to address the reader's concerns, biases, and expectations.

non-scorable: The code "NS" will appear on the student answer document for responses that are written in a language other than English, off-topic, illegible, unintelligible, or otherwise non-responsive to the writing task.

* *Conventions of the English language refer to grammar, punctuation, spelling, capitalization, and usage.*

This guide describes the attributes of student writing at each score point. Each paper receives the score that best fits the overall evidence provided by the student in response to the prompt. However, papers that do not meet the standard for conventions at a 4 or a 3 score point receive a score that is at most one point lower.

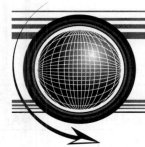

Appendices

Answer Key to the Practice Test

Item #	Standard	Correct Answer	Item #	Standard	Correct Answer
1	10RW1.2	D	31	10RW1.1	D
2	10RL3.1	C	32	10RL3.5	C
3	10RL3.4	C	33	10RW1.1	C
4	10RC2.5	B	34	10RW1.1	D
5	10RL3.5	A	35	10RL3.10	B
6	10RL3.7	D	36	10RL3.3	D
7	10RL3.7	B	37	10RW1.1	B
8	10RL3.8	C	38	10RW1.2	D
9	10RL3.9	A	39	10RC2.7	C
10	10RC2.4	C	40	10RC2.4	D
11	10RC2.5	A	41	8RC2.1	D
12	10RC2.7	C	42	10RW1.1	A
13	10RC2.4	B	43	10RC2.5	B
14	10RC2.7	A	44	8RL3.7	B
15	10RC2.8	D	45	10RL3.12	A
16	10RL3.3	C	46	10WS1.2	C
17	10RL3.6	C	47	10WS1.2	A
18	10RL3.11	D	48	10WS1.1	D
19	10RC2.1	C	49	10WC1.3	C
20	10RC2.1	D	50	10WS1.4	B
21	10RC2.1	A	51	10WC1.2	B
22	10RL3.1	B	52	10WS1.1	C
23	10RL3.6	D	53	10WS1.9	A
24	10RL3.8	A	54	10WS1.9	B
25	10RL3.9	A	55	10WS1.4	D
26	10RL3.4	B	56	10WS1.1	D
27	10RC2.8	D	57	10WS1.5	C
28	10RC2.8	C	58	10WS1.9	D
29	10RC2.8	B	59	10WC1.2	D
30	10RC2.8	A	60	10WC1.1	A

Answer Key

Item #	Standard	Correct Answer	Item #	Standard	Correct Answer
61	10WC1.2	B	69	10WC1.2	B
62	10WC1.1	B	70	10WC1.3	C
63	10WS1.2	A	71	10WC1.3	D
64	10WC1.1	B	72	10WC1.3	A
65	10WC1.2	A	Writing Task 1	10WA2.2	~
66	10WC1.1	D	Writing Task 2	10WA2.3	~
67	10WC1.1	B	Writing Task 3	10WA2.4	~
68	10WC1.3	D			

Answer Key to Sample Questions

Page Number	Standard	Correct Answer	Page Number	Standard	Correct Answer
62	10RW1.2	C	88	10WS1.1	C
64	10RW1.1	C	88	10WS1.2	A
69	10RC2.5	B	89	10WS1.9	D
69	10RC2.8	B	91	10WS1.4	B
70	10RC2.4	A	91	10WS1.5	C
70	10RC2.7	A	94	10WC1.2	B
71	10RC2.4	B	95	10WC1.2	C
74	8RC2.1	A	95	10WC1.1	C
74	8RC2.1	C	96	10WC1.1	A
75	10RC2.1	B	96	10WC1.1	A
76	10RC2.1	C	96	10WC1.1	D
76	10RC2.4	C	97	10WC1.2	A
81	10RL3.1	A	97	10WC1.3	D
81	10RL3.5	B	98	10WC1.3	B
84	10RL3.3	D	98	10WC1.3	C
84	10RL3.4	B	98	10WC1.1	C

NOTES

70872-70872 • PDF19

OSP 09 112153
R04-013 503-0029-05 6-07 595M

NOTES

NOTES

NOTES

NOTES

NOTES

NOTES

NOTES

NOTES

NOTES

NOTES

NOTES

NOTES

NOTES